Dear World, How Are You?

Dear World, How Are You?

Toby Little

MICHAEL JOSEPH
an imprint of
PENGUIN BOOKS

MICHAEL JOSEPH

UK | USA | Canada | Ireland | Australia
India | New Zealand | South Africa

Michael Joseph is part of the Penguin Random House group of companies
whose addresses can be found at global.penguinrandomhouse.com.

First published 2016
001

Copyright © Toby Little, 2016

The moral right of the author has been asserted

The recipes in this book are reproduced exactly
as they appear in the original letters, and as such
their reliability cannot be guaranteed.

Set in 13.75/19 pt Adobe Jenson Pro
Typeset by Jouve (UK), Milton Keynes
Printed in Great Britain by Clays Ltd, St Ives plc

A CIP catalogue record for this book is available from the British Library

HARDBACK ISBN: 978–0–718–18338–7
TRADE PAPERBACK ISBN: 978–0–718–18382–0

www.greenpenguin.co.uk

For everybody who helped me with my project and for every child with a big dream.

Toby

INTRODUCTION

Toby's Beginning

Dear World,

This book is about how I started my great adventure of writing to every single country in the world. My mum is going to tell you the story of how it all started.

It is not a proper story, because proper stories should have magical creatures and made-up things in them, and this story is all true. But I think it is also a little bit magical, because when things happen that you never imagined, then that is a little bit like magic, in a different way.

I don't want to spoil what is in the book by telling you lots about it, so read it if you want. I hope you all enjoy the book!

Bye,

Toby (age 7)

Sabine's Beginning

The whole thing started on the 16th of June, 2013. That day, Toby came home from school with a book called *A Letter to New Zealand*. School had given it to him to read with me at home. Toby was five-and-a-half years old, and it was nearly the end of Reception, the first year at school in the UK. The book was a non-fiction book, and it explained how a letter travels – to the post box, in a van, to a sorting centre, on to a plane . . . all the way to a little boy in New Zealand. The book had a map in it, and Toby realized that New Zealand was a long way away. He had only just learned to write, and he asked me if he could write a letter to New Zealand. I didn't actually know anybody there, but I figured that I might be able to ask around and find some-body. Here is how our conversation went:

Toby: 'Mummy, can I write a letter to New Zealand?'
Me: 'Er . . . yes, I think so. I'll need to find some-body first, but I can ask. Would you like me to?'
Toby: 'Yes! Thank you, Mummy, thank you!'
Me: 'Okay, let's do that, then.'
[Pause]
Toby: 'Mummy?'
Me: 'Yes?'
Toby: 'Can I write a letter to every country in the world?'
Me: '. . .!!'

This is the point where I remember lots of thoughts going through my head. How big the world is, how many countries there are, whether it would even be possible to find somebody in every country . . . I decided that this was not a 'yes' or 'no' question. So instead, we sat down and talked about what a 'country' is, and how there are a number of ways to define that word. We searched the internet together, and decided that one obvious way to talk about 'countries' would be by UN membership – 193 countries. That seemed like a lot of letters for a little boy, especially one who had never written a letter before. So I suggested that Toby might want to start small, maybe writing five letters, and seeing how he felt then. Toby thought that was a brilliant idea, and so I turned to the Internet to look for help, and I asked on social media whether any of my friends knew anybody in another country who would be willing to receive a letter from Toby, and respond.

A number of people commented, and we ended up with five addresses – three from the USA, one from France, and one from Australia. It took Toby a week to write these letters, and the first ever letter went to Patricia in Hawaii. Short as it is, it took

him about half an hour to write, and Patricia
kindly responded very quickly.

Letter to Patricia

Hi Patricia,
Are you well? Do you really live in a town called
Volcano? I wish I lived there.
  Bye,
  Toby

Response from Patricia

Dear Toby,
I live on the big island of Hawaii in the state of
Hawaii. We have an active volcano here and a
mountain that gets snow in the winter. Thank you
for your lovely letter.
  Aloha,
  Patricia

  It is a very short letter, but it was perfect as a first
one, because Patricia's hometown 'Volcano' sounded

like a very cool place to live and sparked Toby's imagination. Toby decided to double-check with Patricia about the name, and we also looked it up on the internet. Toby realized that he liked doing 'research' before writing his letter, so that he could ask the questions he wanted to know the answer to. Over time, we worked out the best way to do research with a little boy who was just learning to read and write: I would do the typing on the Internet, and we would first search for the town or city. We were searching for images, rather than text, and Toby would choose whatever he was interested in – creatures, buildings, monuments. We would click on the image, and I would help him work out whether the picture was actually relevant. This was particularly tricky if the text that went with the image was in a foreign language.

Once we knew what the picture was about, Toby decided on the question. 'Have you been to . . .?', or 'What can you see at . . .?' are quite typical questions, but Toby was also interested in school in other countries, the jobs people have, food and local festivals. The next five letters went to Italy, Japan . . . and we have actually forgotten where else, because we never thought anybody would be interested in knowing! Even though Toby had said he wanted to write to every country in the world, at first, he was just writing to anybody who wanted to be his contact. Five letters . . . ten letters . . . fifteen letters. They weren't all to different countries, but after fifteen or so letters, we thought a bit more about which countries Toby really, really wanted to write to. One of those countries was Egypt, so I set out to find somebody, via friends of friends. All along, we took pictures of the letters, and very early on, we started the website, www.writingtotheworld.com. We started the website because we wanted to have a place where we could store the letters, and where Toby's writing partners could find them, should they get lost in the post. But we also started the website because we quickly realized that, by the time the responses came, Toby would have forgotten his questions, so putting the questions and responses together helped him remember, too.

Soon, Toby realized that not all children lived a life that was like his. First, it was all about different languages, different food, different homes, but one day, we got a contact for Somalia. It was the first time I asked Toby to wait a little bit, while I checked out the pictures on the Internet first, and the first time I wondered how to handle the questions Toby might ask. In his letter, Toby wanted to know what he could do to help the children in Somalia, and so we looked for a charity whose work was easy to explain to a five-year-old. ShelterBox not only had a child-friendly website, they also produced books aimed at children, explaining to them the disasters that can happen around the world. We used their books to understand about tsunamis, floods and earthquakes, and Toby decided that he wanted to raise enough money for one 'ShelterBox', just under £600.

After about twenty letters, the summer holidays started, and we knew we had six weeks to explore the world from our home, because we weren't going on holiday. Instead, we played in the garden, went for walks, and Toby wrote letters. I had to go to Germany for a couple of weeks, and Toby wrote a letter to me there. While I was away, I met several people from other countries, and came home with new contacts for Toby.

Many people have asked where all the contacts have come from. Some have thought that Toby just wrote random letters, but that isn't true. Every single letter has gone to a kind person who agreed in advance to be Toby's contact (there are three . . . maybe four exceptions, but we'll come to those throughout the book). And we found them because the world is full of kind people who were willing to help Toby fulfil his dream.

By the time Toby had written about forty letters, it became clear that he had a previously undiscovered stubborn streak, and that he was simply not going to give up, so I decided that the least I could do would be to make sure there would be contacts for Toby to write to, in every country, for as long as he wanted to. By now, friends were asking friends, and every now and then, we came across an individual with lots of contacts. A person who I had worked with fifteen years ago had a friend who helped with a number of contacts, as did the friend's brother-in-law. We have never met these people, but every now and then, I would get a message saying 'I found somebody in the Seychelles', or 'here is Tajikistan'. In addition to the 'Writing to the World Grapevine', I emailed museums in other countries, schools, embassies, conservation agencies and charities. Every now and then, we struck gold, such as when we contacted African Parks in South Africa, and a lovely lady called Dominique responded by forwarding our message to all parks that were part of the group. By the time school started again in September, Toby was well on the way to achieve his mission; in fact, by the middle of September 2013, there were only seven countries missing, and Toby had written over 250 letters, something neither of us would have imagined at the start. All this time, the project had 'ticked along' quietly, running on personal contacts, friends of friends (of friends of friends of friends). Many of Toby's contacts wanted to keep up-to-date with the project, and since we only had the website, we started a Facebook page, which had a membership of about 100 people – friends, family, and previous contacts. On it, we posted successes, shared when letters were coming in, new contacts found, food we had cooked or baked from the recipes people shared with us . . . By then, Toby was so close to achieving his goal that we had no doubt it was only a matter of time.

Suddenly, something changed. Overnight, in late September 2013, we received several hundred messages. The 'Likes' on Facebook grew from 100 to 1,000, then 2,000, then 3,000, in the space of a single day. Newspapers got in touch. We didn't understand what had changed. Finally, we found an innocent little message: 'I posted about your project on reddit, I hope you don't mind!'

Hundreds and hundreds of people wanted to send Toby things, or wanted to be his writing partner. We could track where newspaper articles were appearing by the messages we received, and we tracked many of them down, in English, Spanish, Portuguese, Serbian, Italian, Korean, Russian, Vietnamese, Chinese, Urdu . . . We took a taxi to the local TV station and did an interview for the local news, and Toby did an interview for the BBC World Service, and BBC Radio Sheffield. I remember picking Toby up from school with the question 'there's a reporter from New York who'd like to have a chat with you . . . what do you think?' Life got a bit crazy for a little while. The publisher who had published the original book *A Letter to New Zealand* (Collins Big Cat) wrote to say they would match-fund Toby's first ShelterBox, so that he had now raised over £1,000.

There were a couple of offers from people who wanted to adopt Toby (which we didn't consider!). But above all, there were so, so many heart-warming messages from people all over the world, who were telling us that Toby's project had touched something in them – a belief and hope for a better world. A childlike wonder. The determination to follow a dream. Some messages were deeply personal, many, many apologized for their broken English. But we didn't notice the broken English, we just noticed that so many people wanted to let Toby know they liked his project, and that they had gone through the trouble of getting in touch. Some people wrote in their own language – if we couldn't read it, we got help to translate it, and Toby decided that he wanted to learn lots of languages, so that he could speak to as many people in the world as possible.

We couldn't reply to all the messages, it was impossible, but we read every single one. And so, the Facebook page became a way for us to talk to the world. By now, there were over 5,000 people on there, from all over the world. They were keen to share their world with Toby, but also with each other, and to learn from the letters Toby received back. We would ask what creatures people would find in their homes, and we learned about boomslangs in South Africa and scorpions in Central America. When Toby did a craft fair to raise money for ShelterBox, we asked 'the world' for crafting ideas, and then made woven fish from Thailand. We asked for recipes, and spent weeks cooking and baking.

And all along, the letters continued.

Somewhere in the midst of all of this, in early October 2013, we found the last contact, for San Marino. Toby wrote the letter, and then, he had written to every country in the world. He was done. Mission accomplished.

Or was it?

Toby said at the beginning that this isn't a proper story, because it isn't made up. But it isn't a proper story for another reason. At school, Toby is learning that stories should have a beginning, a middle and an end. This, right now, would be a great point for a happy end. Except it wasn't a happy end. It was a happy middle. Because Toby didn't want to stop writing.

When Toby celebrated his sixth birthday in November 2013, I asked the world to help me with a surprise, and people from all over the world took pictures of themselves with a note saying 'Happy Birthday, Toby' – most notably, James and his colleagues, who painted a huge banner and stood at the South Pole with it.

Toby now needs less help with his research from me. His handwriting progression can be traced through hundreds of letters – the beginnings of joined-up writing, the curly phase. If we have one regret, it's that Toby never put dates on the letters. Certain letters can be traced to specific events – his letter to Syria (another country where I checked the pictures first) was written days after the gas attacks in 2013. Throughout the letters, many references are made to natural disasters. The project has had a side-effect, too. Whenever anything happens in the world – anywhere at all – we know somebody there. When Typhoon Haiyan hit the Philippines in November 2013, we received updates from Anika and her students, telling us that they were okay. Toby is still fundraising, and every time he receives a letter that tells him that a ShelterBox has gone to a disaster area, he is happy that he has been able to help a bit. All disasters are personal, each and every one of them has a name, a story, a letter attached to it.

We are writing this in November 2015. At the time of writing, Toby has written 562 letters, but by the time you hold this book in your hands, it will probably be more. If you ask Toby how long he wants to continue, he currently says 'until I'm a grown-up'. He might get up tomorrow and declare that he's done, for ever, and that would be absolutely fine, too. But he doesn't think that he will. When Toby started the project, he said he did it 'to learn more about the world, to help people understand each other better, and to make the world a better place'. Since then, he has also said that he wants to 'show people how amazing the world is'. We could not have imagined the kindness of all the people involved in his project, his contacts, those who helped find them, and the people who have taken part in it on the Facebook page. You are what makes the project possible, what makes the story magical. Thank you. Thank you so, so much, from both of us.

I wrote this introduction after lots of conversations with Toby, where we discussed what he wanted to share with you, and he then read what I wrote, and made suggestions for any changes he wanted to make. The same is true for the stories that introduce the letters in this book. In sharing these letters with you, we tried to balance the continents, the ages of contacts and the topics – we could have chosen other letters, and Toby loves all of them, not just the ones published here. We have boxes of letters in our home, and as Toby is continuing to write, almost every week brings new letters, new questions, new connections and new explorations. Thank you for joining us on this journey.

Sabine, Toby's mum

EUROPE

Austria

*Really we have Stefan and Katja to thank for
all the cooking and baking we have done as part of
the project. They sent us a recipe for Sachertorte and
the rest, as they say, is history! Now Toby very often
asks for a recipe, and we have lost count of the number
of things we have tasted from all over the world!*

Letter to Stefan and Katja

Hi Stefan and Katja,
How are you? We saw pictures of Graz. What is inside the Kunsthaus? It looks really funny!
   Bye,
   Toby

Response from Stefan and Katja

Dear Tobi,
Sorry that we write so late but we have been in England for 3 weeks and came back on the 29th of July. We are fine, thanks. How are you? At the moment we have got 39° in Austria.
   Here is a recipe for a traditional dessert called Sachertorte.

Recipe for Sachertorte

Cake:
130g semisweet cooking chocolate
130g soft butter

40g icing sugar

5g vanilla sugar

1 pinch salt

6 egg yolks

6 egg whites

180g granulated sugar

130g flour

Icing:

400g apricot jam

Chocolate icing (finished product)

Zubereitung [method]:

For the Sachertorte, preheat oven to 190° C. Melt the semisweet chocolate in a water bath while stirring. Allow to cool. Mix the butter, icing sugar, vanilla sugar and salt. Mix until frothy and add the yolks one after the other. Beat the egg whites with the sugar until firm, sift the flour. Carefully fold in the egg white and flour alternately into the chocolate mixture. Grease the cake pan with butter and dust with flour. Fill in the pan and bake in the oven for approximately 60 minutes. Sprinkle granulated sugar on the baking paper, turn out the cake onto it and allow to cool.

Cut the cake horizontally into two layers and coat with half the jam, then put together again. Heat the remaining jam and spread thinly all over the cake. Warm the chocolate icing according to instructions and ice the cake.

Tip:
It is best to prepare the cake on the previous day and to keep in the refrigerator overnight. Sacher-torte is traditionally served with whipping cream.

Cyprus

Stanna is a very lovely lady who got in touch after Toby's project went viral. Toby wrote to her and her partner, Koullis, just before their wedding. When the response came, it included some wedding photos, as well as a little box with a piece of wedding cake!

Letter to Stanna and Koullis

Dear Stanna and Koullis,

How are you? What does an archaeological engineer do? Can you visit Salamis? Do people still dig there? What is it like living in Cyprus? I hope you have a happy wedding. I'm sorry about your car crash. How do you move now?

Bye,
Toby

Response from Stanna

Dear Toby & family,

Thank you so much for your letter. Your writing is very good. You must be getting much better with all your practice at letter writing! What an interesting project you have.

I will tell you a little about myself. I am originally from England but I have travelled all over the world working as an archaeological engineer, and that is how I ended up living in Cyprus 23 years ago. I live in a small village called Liopetri, which means 'little stones'.

I have been busy planning my wedding, which is on Saturday. I am marrying my best friend. He is a Cypriot and looks after me a lot, which is very good as I had a bad car accident last year. I was in hospital for 6 months, then in a wheelchair for another 6 months, but I had 2 operations to rebuild the broken bones in my neck and back and I am now walking with sticks or in a neck collar.

I am trying to exercise every day by swimming and kayaking, which I enjoy and I do at the *potamos*. *Potamos* means river in Greek – which is the language spoken in Cyprus. Does it sound like a word you know? Yes! Hippopotamus! And that is where the word comes from originally. A hippopotamus is *ippos* (horse) and *potamos* (river) – a river horse. Hippos are a bit fat to be called horses I think, though. Do you? Maybe we should add the word *vasha*, which means fat!

My job used to mean that I got to go to all the places people were going to build where there was archaeology. Do you know what archaeology is? It's where we get to study things that are old – sometimes they are buried in the ground, like bones and stones, or sometimes they already exist where we can see them, like pyramids or ruins in caves. It is very interesting work. My job was very good because when I started I was the first person to do it! Now there are lots and it's more fun (the engineering part not the archaeology!).

I also write books and magazines. I hope Mummy and Daddy like the one I have sent you. It is all about wine in Cyprus.

So sorry for the delay in writing to you. My neck broke again; I go for another operation in 2 days. I will be able to walk and write. I got married, and was doing well until the break so hopefully I will be better like that again ☺

Lots of love,

Stanna

Denmark

Toby has written several letters to Denmark, and every single one could have been included in the book. We chose Laura's because it is one of the more recent ones, but also because it is from a slightly lesser-known area of the country. Also, we loved how she described Denmark through the eyes of somebody who had recently moved there and fallen in love with the place.

Letter to Laura

Dear Laura,

How are you? Have you been to Lindholm Høje? It looks amazing. Can you go inside the *Springeren* submarine? Have you stood inside the Water Pavilion? What is your favourite Danish food? Does it get really cold in winter?

Bye,

Toby

Response from Laura

Dear Toby,

How are you? I am fine and really happy to hear from you. First, I want to answer all your questions then I'll tell you something more.

Yes, I've been to Lindholm Høje and it's as amazing as it looks, especially if you're lucky enough to go there on a sunny day. I want to go back there next weekend, as it's going to be a Viking festival and I surely don't want to miss that! I've never seen one before so I'm really looking forward ☺

If you ever come here you'll be able to go inside

the submarine or climb on one of the tanks and you'll hear thrilling stories. (Everybody speaks English here, so it won't be difficult.)

But, unfortunately, I have not been able to go inside the Water Pavilion yet. I moved to Aalborg only recently and the museum is under renovation right now. I'll have to wait for this autumn to go there. If I go inside the Water Pavilion, I'll send you a picture, promise.

However, I've been inside the fountain you see on the postcard I'm sending you. On it you can see some of my favourite spots of Aalborg, although Østre Anlæg (a city park) is not shown. I was also looking for a postcard with some Danish food but I found none. I'm still trying to discover Danish cuisine but, up to now, my favourite recipe is creamed chicken with white asparagus. It tastes much better than it looks! And I do like rhubarb a lot!

As I told you, I moved here recently because of my job (I am a population geneticist, working mainly in conservation). So I left Sardinia (Italy) for Aalborg. My colleagues here say winter is not so cold here, with temperatures around 5° C and not so much snow. Well, I must confess I'm not so confident in their forecast; Danish spring was

Sardinian winter, so . . . I really hope I will not freeze this winter!

However, if we don't consider the weather, Aalborg is a lovely place to live. There are several museums and many activities for people of all ages. Last month there was a guided tour where they explained sea life in the fiord to children. Every year, the university students present their invention to the public and so do the art students. There is also a quite nice park close to the Culture Centre, where all the artists (Sting, Elton John, Bocelli and many others) planted a tree. It's a nice initiative, made even nicer by the small speakers close to the tree that play some of the artist's most famous songs. And every now and then there are small festivals + markets with traditional things from specific countries (Italy) or continents (Asia). I love them and I hope there are going to be more.

Every year, on the 23rd June, they have big bonfires with music and speeches to celebrate the longest day of the year. It was amazing, with so many people and the sunset at 10.30 p.m.

But one thing I'm really looking forward to is the 'Tall Ship Race'. It's a sail race and you can even join the crew and take part in the race! It must be great to sail in one of those big ships!! I never sailed but doing it in one of these ships looks like being a pirate for a day! ☺

I hope I successfully described you my new home as I'm falling in love with it. I wish I shared some of its beauty and charm with you!

Have a great time and keep EXPLORING! ☺

Wish you all the best (to Mum and Dad too, of course),

Laura

France

Like Denmark, we have quite a few letters to choose from in France! Toby has just started learning French, and so it won't be long now before some French words will start creeping into his letters.

Letter to Nathalie

Dear Nathalie,

How are you? Why is Pont Neuf called New Bridge when it is 500 years old? What are the two buildings on the coat of arms? Have you been to the Cité de l'espace? Why is Toulouse called the Pink City?

Bye,

Toby

Response from Nathalie

Hi Toby,

I'm very pleased to have received a letter from you.

Excuse me respond a little late but I live 30km from Toulouse and I had to find a way to collect postcards.

I've got 2 children: one girl who is 18 years old and a boy who is 12 years old. We have got 2 cats and we live in the countryside.

I'll try to answer your question on Toulouse. Toulouse is known as the pink city because the buildings are built of bricks that can be baked or unbaked clay. When you are on a plane, the old town is pink. Surrounding, some other cities are built in the same way, as for example Albi, which is listed as World Heritage of UNESCO. I've gone to the Cité de l'espace but it was a long time ago, when it opened. I've good memories because you can see a Soyuz and an Ariane. You also have a planetarium and lot of things to visit. It's like an amusement park but very specialized.

You can find more informations about it on the internet.

Le Pont Neuf is not a new bridge but paradoxically it is the oldest one. It dates from 1632 and was inaugurated by King Louis XIV, called the Sun King (he was living in Versailles). Other bridges were built but they were swept away by floods. The Garonne was very dangerous at this time. The people of Toulouse have kept the habit of calling it the 'Pont Neuf' even [if] it's not true. It is strange, isn't it? This was transmitted from generation to generation.

The coat of arms has two buildings. One was destroyed: it was the castle named le Château Narbonnais. In the eleventh century it was the home of the counts of Toulouse. Built on the

Roman boundary wall of the eleventh century, the venerable house of the Raymond counts was a powerful fortress to protect Toulouse, with a perfect view of the River Garonne and visibility towards people arriving at the door of the city. It was razed in the sixteenth century. The castle, at least its bases, is now more than 3 meters from the ground. The archaeologists found its bases during development works of Toulouse. In its place there's now the courthouse, but inside we can see the bases of the Château Narbonnais. The second monument is the basilica of Saint Sernin. It's on the right on the coat of arms. This is one of the most famous buildings of the city. It houses the relics of St Saturnin, the first bishop of Toulouse, who was martyred in 250 AD. Saint Sernin is the largest Romanesque church preserved in Europe. Its dimensions are: 115m long and 64m wide. It's half built with stone and brick (the first material was expensive so they preferred using bricks).

Toulouse is also known for a plant, the violet, with which we make bouquets, perfumes, sweets.

Toby, I hope that you can understand me because my English needs to be improved! I hope that someday you'll be travelling in countries from where you've received letters. It'll be fantastic.

But, for this time, what you do is wonderful because you come into contact with the world without *a priori.*

Continue to do it because you get enriched day after day.

Kindly,

Nathalie

Germany

Toby's very first contact in Germany was Sabine, but it seemed a bit of a cheat to include that! Toby's more recent letters to Germany are all written in German, as his language skills improve. Until Toby wrote to Astrid, he had never heard of the job title 'glaciologist'.

Letter to Astrid

Dear Astrid,

How are you? Which is your favourite glacier in the world? Why do glaciers move? What is the best thing about living in Immenstadt? Can you swim in the Alpsee?

   Bye,
   Toby

Response from Astrid

Dear Toby,

Sorry I am a bit late answering your letter, because I had a busy October and I also was a bit lazy and enjoyed the nice autumn weather with my sister, hiking in the mountains. That's the good thing about living here. You can walk in the mountains, go climbing, bicycling and swimming.

   The first snow has already fallen on the mountains a few days ago, so it is much too cold for swimming now. But in summertime you can go swimming in the lake. The water temperature reaches more than 20° C. The lake is more than

3km long so you can also go for surfing or sailing if the wind is good (mostly in spring and autumn).

I am living outside the city in a small village nearby. There I can have a small garden and I like growing flowers and my own vegetables. Now I have to prepare the garden for the coming winter-time. I tie up some of the plants so that the snow does not crush them down.

In wintertime you can do every kind of winter sport you like in the region and I like snow very much. That's the reason I am working in glaciology. Snow and ice is something special and fascinating. There are some nice books from Kenneth George Libbrecht about snowflakes with lots of pictures because every snow crystal looks different. Maybe you can have a look at the books in a library.

I do not have one favorite glacier. All glaciers have something special and are unique. A week ago we were at the Schwarzmilzferner. It is a very small glacier (150,000sqm) not far from my home (30km distance). We go there twice a year.

In springtime we look how much snow has fallen over the wintertime by digging a snow pit and in autumn we measure how much snow and ice was melted during the summertime. So we can say something about the mass balance of the glacier for the year. Within the last ten years the glacier melted about 15m and also it reduces in size.

Ice in a way behaves like honey: it moves very slowly if you place it on a slope. If you put some honey on an inclined breakfast plate, it will start moving downwards. The same happens to glacier ice, if it is on a mountain slope. The warmer the ice or the steeper the slope, the faster the glacier will flow. Usually glaciers flow some tens to hundred meters per year. The fastest glaciers in the world (Jakobshavn Glacier, Helheim Glacier, Columbia Glacier . . .), however, flow 15–20 km/year, or 40–55 m/day. It is almost possible to see them move.

There are many other interesting things about glaciers and I hope you will find out more in the future. In my opinion nature can show you many wonderful things and ideas and it is good to be curious and investigative. Good luck for your future!

Astrid

Iceland

Every single response Toby has received from Iceland has been wonderful. In December 2014 we were able to go for a brief trip over Christmas and Toby finally saw the Northern Lights himself, after asking about them in so many letters!

Letter to Iggy

Dear Iggy,
How are you? Have you been to the Church of Hallgrímur? Have you seen the *Sun Voyager* or the Northern Lights?
    Bye,
    Toby

Response from Iggy

Dear Toby,
The answer is three times yes! I've seen all the things you ask about and I see them regularly.
    The church of Hallgrímur plays a big role in my life. It's my parish church. I stand in the church choir for 16 years and I met my wife in that choir too! We got married in the church and our children are christened and confirmed there too. The church has a huge organ and in the tower there are bells that can be played from a keyboard inside the church.
    The *Sun Voyager* is only 2 minutes away from my house (like the church) and I really like it! I pass it

44

at the beginning of my route when I go out jogging. It is a popular stop among tourists and I'm sure it is one of the most photographed spots in the whole of Reykjavik.

The Northern Lights are an amazing phenomenon! Constantly moving in the sky and changing colors. I've seen them a few times from my garden, but it is best to go deep into the country where there are no electric lights around. There you also see billions of stars much more clearly!

Best regards and good luck with your project,

Iggy

Malta

Malta has been wonderful to Toby. When his project went viral, lots and lots of Maltese people got in touch – so many, in fact, that we joked that Toby would be able to stand at a street corner in Malta and be recognized. That's probably not true, but the responses he has received from Malta are all equally amazing. Francesca's response showed him how fiendishly difficult Maltese is!

Letter to Francesca

Dear Francesca,
How are you? Have you been swimming in the sea? Why is Maltese hard to learn? Can you write a sentence in Maltese for us? Which country that you travelled to was your favourite? Which country are you going to next?
    Bye,
    Toby

Response from Francesca

Dear Toby,
Thank you for choosing to write to me. I was very excited to receive your letter in the post.
    Since Malta is an island surrounded by the Mediterranean Sea and because we have very hot summers, swimming in the sea is one of my favourite things to do to cool off in summer. Unfortunately the sea is very cold and rough at this time of the year, so I have not yet managed to have my first swim of 2015.
    Maltese is a very special language; this is because throughout history Malta was ruled by a lot of

countries, including the Arabs, the Romans, the French and the British. Every ruler left their own special touch on our language. So it is hard for some people to learn it because it is a big mixture of languages. As Maltese this is good because it means that we understand little bits of many languages.

If I wanted to say 'My name is Francesca' in Maltese I would say *'Jiena jisimni Francesca'*. In Maltese the letter 'j' has the same sound as the letter 'y' in English. So you can say *'Jiena jisimni Toby u nieħu gost nikteb ittri lik nies madwar id-dinja'*. The 'ħ' has the same sound as a normal 'h' in English and the sentence means 'My name is Toby and I enjoy writing letters to people around the world'.

To answer your question about which country was my favourite, I had to think a lot because every country is unique and special in its own way and I always find it difficult to choose just one place. So far I would say that my three favourite places are San Francisco in North America, Rome and St Petersburg in Europe, and Abu Dhabi in the Middle East.

At the end of March I am going to visit Chiang

Mai in Thailand. I am very excited about this trip because there is an elephant reserve not far from the hotel that I will be staying at.

Bye,

Francesca

Norway (Svalbard)

A letter from Svalbard may not represent
'typical' Norway, but Toby was absolutely fascinated
to read that it is a place where many children have
seen a polar bear, every family has a snow
scooter, and fossils are all around. The class sent
a delicate fossilized leaf, which is beautiful!

Letter to Longyearbyen School

Dear everybody,
How are you? Do you have sledge dogs? Do you get
any polar bears? Have you found any fossils? What
is your school like? What food do you eat?
Bye,
Toby

Response from pupils at Longyearbyen School

Dear Toby,
Thank you much for your letter. It was nice to get a
letter from you. How are you doing?
We go in the 2 class at Longyearbyen School.
We are 22 pupils: 11 girls and 11 boys. School
begins at 8:15 and ends at 12:15 and after that
some of us go to after-school care.
None of us has sledge dogs, but 5 of us have dogs
and 8 have already been dog sledding.
There are many polar bears on Svalbard. The
majority in our class has already seen polar bears or
polar bears' tracks. Philip has seen a polar bear
outside their hut. The polar bear is one of the most

dangerous animals on earth. Polar bears are normally not in town. They eat seals.

When we go on tour we must have a rifle and a signal pistol with us.

Everyone in the class has a snow scooter in the family.

There are 2,500 people living on Svalbard, here in town around 2,000. There is one school with 270 pupils.

Almost everyone in the class has found fossil. The mountains on Svalbard are filled with coal and fossils. Ingvild has found a fossil that you can have.

We take a lunch box with us at school and we get fruits from the school. Those who go to after-school care get a meal there 3 times a week. It is warm. We have made a list about what we like to eat: crispbread with cheese or bacon or ham or caviar cream or liver pâté or nougat cream, noodle salad, noodles, lasagne, pizza, tacos, pancakes, porridge, beef, hamburger, meatballs, fish balls, chicken.

We hope you are doing fine.

Greetings from the northernmost town in the world.

Serbia

We didn't know Tatjana until the project; now we are in regular contact with her online. She translated and sent a whole children's book, and ended up on the radio in Serbia when the project went viral – she sent us a link to the recording, and it was one of the rare occasions where we got to hear the voice of one of Toby's writing partners!

Letter to Tatjana

Hi Tatjana,
How are you? Have you been to the fortress? Do you know why there are tanks there? Have you ever swum in the Danube?
Bye,
Toby

Postcards from Tatjana

Hi Toby!
I enjoy participating in your Writing to the World project ☺ Our world is an interesting place, so many beautiful places and people!

Beograd (Belgrade) is the capital and largest city of Serbia, located at the confluence of Sava and Danube (we say Dunav here) rivers. I don't swim in Danube but I do love swimming in the city lake, at Ada Cioganlija.

Hope you and your mum visit us sometime in the future.
☺ Tatjana

*

Our fortress, Kalemegdan, is very old. Built by a
Celtic tribe and then Romans, centuries BC it was
known as Singidunum.

The fortress represent old citadel and the lovely
Kalemegdan Park. You saw the tanks because there
is a military museum there, and also there is a
museum of forestry and hunting and the Belgrade
Zoo.

*

Greetings from Belgrade, Serbia!
Hope you get lots of postcards from all over the
world!!!

Sweden

Writing to Annali was the first time we read about the European City of Culture, and Toby wrote the letter in 2013, just before Umeå took that title in 2014. We looked at past European Cities of Culture and found they got decided a long time in advance! Toby's letter to Annali was also the first time he considered indigenous people outside the USA and Canada. We loved looking up the Sami culture and language in our research.

Letter to Annali

Dear Annali,
How are you? How often do you see the Northern
Lights? Do you know any Sami people? Why is
Umeå the European Capital of Culture?
    Bye,
    Toby

Response from Annali

Hej Toby!
I am doing quite well. Hope all is well with you too!
    It is getting darker and colder here in Umeå,
Sweden, every day. Today the sunset was at 14:20! I
see the Northern Lights a fair amount but I wish I
saw them every night. When it is clear and dark
out and the colors of the lights dance in the sky it is
truly magical and breathtaking.
    I know a few people of Sami heritage; they are a
rich culture and the only group of people I know
that have real reindeer! Pretty cool! The European
Capital of Culture is working to teach people more
about northern Sweden and the unique qualities of

Sweden. It should be fun with a lot of tourism, music and sports!

I like the peacefulness of Sweden in winter right at sunset when everything gets a bit more quiet and the light makes the snow sparkle. It is a bit early but at least this card should reach you in time for Christmas! It says 'Merry Christmas and Happy New Year! Enjoy the holidays!'

Continue chasing your dreams, Toby, it is an admirable and desired quality. Always keep a passion for life and, most of all, love loud & enjoy life!

Hällsningar,

Annali

United Kingdom

At the time of writing Toby has written twenty-three letters to people in the UK – how can we possibly choose one? Many of the people Toby writes to within the UK are specialists, working as archaeologists, disaster specialists, aid workers or authors. Some have even shared research with us that has not been published yet, so we can't use those! Instead we have chosen to share two letters with you – one from Andrew, who works as an archaeologist in Northern Ireland, and whose suggestion on naming trowels came the very day that we went out to buy a trowel for Toby to take on a fossil-hunting holiday, and one from Chrystal, because Toby's letter to her, and her response, sparked wonderful contributions on Toby's Facebook page from people sharing sculptural walking trails from all over the world – and Toby wants to do them all.

Letter to Andrew

Dear Andrew,
How are you? What is your favourite find ever?
What is your favourite find from Dunluce Castle?
Have you been to a different country to do archae-
ology? How many people work on the dig? If I get a
trowel, what should I name it?
 Bye,
 Toby

Response from Andrew

Dear Toby,
It was very nice to receive your letter; I'm doing
well, thanks.
 'What is your favourite find?' is a hard question
for an archaeologist! Although one that sticks in
mind is when I found a Bronze Age burial inside a
stone-lined grave (we call it a cist). It was very
exciting to look inside and see the remains of a
person along with a pottery bowl left by their loved
ones, which hadn't been seen or touched by anyone
for 4,000 years or more.

At Dunluce I think my favourite find is what we call the merchant's seal – it's a metal object with an image carved on one end, which would have been used to leave an impression on the sealing wax of official documents. It's around 400 years old. Maybe you could use one to seal your letters?

I've never worked on an archaeological dig outside of Ireland. Although when I'm on holiday I often drag my poor wife around archaeological sites just for fun. You never really switch off as an archaeologist, but it can be difficult to get your trowel through airport security.

Archaeological digs can be very small – carried out by just one archaeologist – or in some cases dozens of archaeologists can work on the same site. At Dunluce we tend to have around ten archaeologists working on a dig, but we're planning for larger digs in future and we'll be hoping to have members of the public joining in as volunteers. Keep an eye out and maybe in a few years you could end up being a volunteer archaeologist at Dunluce.

I hope you get the chance to have your own trowel some day. Naming it is an important and very personal matter – the choice will have to be yours. Maybe you could be inspired by how the Vikings used to name their swords? If you ever want to try out archaeology there should be a local branch of the Young Archaeologists' Club close to where you live – maybe you could look them up?

Nice hearing from you, and best of luck with your letters.

Best wishes,
Andrew
Dunluce Project Archaeologist, DOE: Historic Environment Division

*

Letter to Chrystal

Dear Chrystal,
How are you? Did you see the Gromit statues in Bristol when they were there? We found all fifty book benches in London last year. What is your job? Have you driven across the Clifton Suspension Bridge? Will you go to the Balloon Fiesta?

Bye,
Toby

Dear Toby,

Greetings from Bristol!!

Thank you very much for your letter. I feel very honoured to have received it as I have been a fan of your letter writing for a long time.

I am sorry it took a few weeks to reply to you. I have three children and I needed to wait for the summer holidays to start before I had a chance to write!

In answer to your questions: I do have a job. I work in my children's primary school where I am training to be a teaching assistant. I work a lot with children with special educational needs. The work is hard but lots of fun. As I am still training, I go to college every Friday to learn how to do my job in better ways. I also work for a financial advisor. Finally, I have my own craft business where I turn old books, which are going to be destroyed, into works of art for people. This is called book folding. It is lots of fun and at least the books are recycled.

I have driven across the Clifton Suspension Bridge and I have walked across it. The view from the middle is amazing, although it can be scary on a windy day! Near to the suspension bridge is a smooth rock slide. Over the years so many people have slid down a certain piece of rock that it is now as smooth as a piece of glass!

The Balloon Fiesta is lots of fun, especially the Nightglow. At night-time, as the sun sets, there are many balloons that are tethered to the ground and they fill up their canopies with hot air. Music then plays and the balloons have their flames lit in time to the music. It is like they are dancing! The Balloon Fiesta is usually on the weekend closest to my birthday. I am not sure if we will make it this year as this summer holiday is rather busy. At least we will see the balloons floating over the house throughout the weekend!

When the Gromit statues came to Bristol we had so much fun trying to find them all! Two years before the Gromits, we had gorillas. They were auctioned to raise money for the zoo. The Gromits were used to raise money for the children's hospital. This year we have Shaun the Sheep! We have managed to find 4 sheep so far, including my favourite one. It is called Buddleia and has been painted so it looks covered in buddleia flowers and butterflies! It is beautiful! They also had Shauns in London, although there will be more in Bristol. I looked up the benches; they sound amazing!

Thank you so very much for taking the time to write to me. I think you are doing an amazing thing.

Lots of love,

Chrystal x

NORTH AMERICA

Bahamas

When Toby wrote to the then headmaster of St Andrew's School in the Bahamas, he received back a huge parcel of postcards, written by 'Dr. C', teachers and students. It was such an explosion of colour; it felt like they had brought the Bahamas to us in Sheffield!

Letter to Dr Canterford

Dear Dr Canterford,
How are you? Why is Cat Island called Cat Island?
Have you ever been to the Marine Habitat at the
Atlantis? Have you been to Preacher's Cave? What
is your school like?
Bye,
Toby

**Response from Dr Canterford and St Andrew's
School**

Hi Toby,
I hope you like all of the postcards from the Bahamas. I have been here 2 yrs now + really like it. If
you ever make it here we would be happy to show
you around our school. I hope you get lots of other
cards from around the world.
With best wishes,
Dr. C (This is what my students call me!!)

*

Hello Toby,
My name is Ms Tilney and I am a teacher at

St Andrew's School in Nassau the Bahamas.
We have a swimming pool, a big hall, lots of playgrounds and classrooms too. The sun shines a lot
here and it rains a lot too. The sea is very beautiful
and the children at school are happy. I come from a
place called Norwich in England.

From,

Ms Tilney

*

Dear Toby,

I have never been to the Marine Habitat at Atlantis
but my children (Marley, 4, and Charlotte, 1) go to
the beach every weekend. Marley is learning to
swim and loves snorkelling. Sometimes I have
trouble getting him out of the water. Charlotte
loves the beach too but she is afraid of seaweed!

Best wishes from the Bahamas,

Rachael

*

Dear Toby,

My name is Adam. Life in the Bahamas is
really cool. It is a cool place to live but it is
really hot.

Joby

*

Hello Toby,
It's really cool to live here because there is not really tall buildings.
    Sincerely,
    Adam

*

Hi Toby,
I'm from the Bahamas. It's really cool how you're sending postcards to everyone in the world! My name is Alexander. You can call me Alex for short.
    Your friend,
    Alex

*

Dear Toby,
The Bahamas has the cleanest ocean in the world. Also the deepest blue hole in Long Island, Bahamas. Our school is awesome too. It has lots of kids and nice teachers too. Life in the Bahamas is very awesome. Also we go to the beach every Sunday. A fact is that we have a big paradise called Alandise. It is awesome too. I love the Bahamas!!
    From,
    Joshua

Canada

We loved researching Shaun's letter, which led us to the First Nations of Canada. As well as his own response and those of his students, Shaun spent a long time commenting on posts on the Writing to the World Facebook page, sharing more of his life and culture. He sent us two recipes, one for bannock and the other for moose stew — we made the bannock almost straight away, but have not yet tackled the moose!

Letter to Shaun

Dear Shaun,
How are you? What is it like living in two cultures? Could you live without going shopping? What food and medicine do you hunt for? Is Chief Brian Ladue your dad? What movies do you want to write?
  Bye,
  Toby

Response from Shaun

Dentae Toby:
I live part-time in Vancouver, BC, which is a very big city, and I live in Ross River, which is a small village surrounded by forests, mountains, rivers and lakes. In Vancouver there are a lot of people, not many forests or wild animals. You asked about Brian Ladue, the chief of the Ross River Dena Council; he is my nephew, my only sister's oldest son. I am very proud of him.
  I am teaching writing and art at the local school until Nov. 22nd, then I return to Vancouver. I told

my students about you and they wanted to write to
you. So I have enclosed all their letters. They are
very curious about you and how you live too.
I have started writing my first movie. It's a love
story. I hope to write a science-fiction story next. I
like all kinds of movies.

    Take care,
    Shaun

*

Dear Toby,
My name is Daniel. I live in Ross River. It's great
living here. How is it where you live? It must be
good for you because you are having a birthday.
You will be 6 years old. Happy birthday! We have
wolves here. They are like big dogs. They are very
mean. They also hunt in packs. We don't have the
same birds as you. What do you have? The internet
is fast here. I like playing games and playing outside. I am in grade 6. I also hunt caribou with a
30.30 cal. in the winter. I drive a quad. It's very fast.
How is it to live in the city? This is a Kaska word
[that] means see you later: *nahganastanzi*.

    D.
    P.S. Cool Beans

*

Dear Toby,

How are you? I'm good. My name is Michael. I'm 12 years old, and I'm in grade 7. Happy birthday, Toby. I live in the Yukon in Ross River, YT. It is cold where I live. It is about to snow in Ross River. Ross River is a very small town. Mostly all my family goes out in the bush to hunt animals like moose, geese, grouse. In Ross River kids are allowed to drive snowmobiles and quads. This summer Ross River got flooded by the river and some people's houses were flooded. We have a school and it is called Ross River School. It is a small school. There about 50 to 100 kids in this school.

This is a Kaska word in my language: *nahga-nastanzi*. That means see you later.

By Michael

*

Dear Toby,

How are you? I'm good. My name is Jared. I'm turning 11 years old, and I'm in grade 6. In Ross River it's kind of boring. Our teacher name is Ms Etzel. My grandma and my grandpa is famous. I Live in Yukon. I almost got killed by cow moose in 2012. I'll tell you about Ross River – not that much to tell you. Our school is a lot of fun.

We have 44 students and sometimes there's wolves in our town. They always kill dogs. Don't be afraid of wolves. It's simple to scare wolves. You have to use big antlers, put on light, make yourself big and tall, show it to them. They will run away. That's all. Much to tell you, I hope you could come – I'll teach you to scare wolves.

By Jared

*

Dear Toby,

My name is Danika and I am 12 years old, and I am in grade 7. It is very fun down here in Ross River and there is 352 people in the community and there is also 44 students in the school. This is a very small community unlike England. The nearest city is 5 hours away from Ross River to White-horse. It is very fun up in the bush and there is a lot of animals in the bush. There is a lot of kinds of animals like moose, wolves, groundhogs, grouse, marten, lynx, caribou, and there is only one store in Ross River and one gas station.

Nahganastanzi,
Danika

Dominica

When Lisette's letter arrived, it was covered
in beautiful animal stamps, and when we heard
of the 365 rivers on Dominica, Toby quickly decided
that it would be wonderful to visit one each
day for a whole year – but maybe that is a
project that'll have to wait a while . . .

Letter to Lisette

Hi Lisette,
How are you? Did you see *Pirates of the Caribbean* being filmed? What is it like living near so many active volcanoes? What is your job?
   Bye,
   Toby

Response from Lisette

Dear Toby,
I owe you a huge apology. I should have written to you a long time ago. I have been very busy as I own a real estate company here in Dominica. I also am an artist and have been painting our indigenous parrots the Sisserou and the Jaco.

   Toby, the Caribbean is where all the pirates used to come and where the famous film *Pirates of the Caribbean* was filmed. We live on the island of Dominica, which gets confused with the Dominican Republic. Dominica is made up of 9 dormant volcanoes, so her name is Waitukubuli, which means 'how tall is her body'.

Dominica is known as the jewel in the crown of all the islands as she is beautiful and, unlike any other island in the Windies, Dominica has 365 rivers! We have the most amazing waterfalls and a great deal of springs so we have our own water supply. This makes the island very lush and we can grow anything on the island. We also have Boiling Lake, which is made up from the sulphur from the earth. We are so lucky as we have quite a lot of hot pools, which are fantastic to swim in or just relax and chill out in like a hot bath!

Back in the 19th century Dominica used to produce a lot of the lime for Rose's Lime Juice. For many years, until just recently, we used to grow and sell bananas. The bananas here at the moment have a disease black stickacoa (not sure of the spelling we have no internet today!!).

My husband, Laurie, and I live in the Layou Valley close to the Layou River. The river is one of the largest in Dominica and the tourists come to go tubing and swimming in the river, especially off the cruise ships. We have a lot of cruise ships visiting us in the tourist season, which is from November to April 6 months. One of the reasons we only have a tourist season for 6 months is because from June to November we have the hurricane season! We do not have hurricanes every year, thank goodness, but it can happen that we can have one sometimes. The yachts all go to the Mediterranean in the summer months so they are not in danger from hurricanes in the Caribbean.

Where we live is in the middle of the countryside; we own 3 acres of land and grow a lot of fruit. We love the limes especially. It is great to have breakfast eating our own bananas, pineapples, papaya, grapefruit and oranges. We have a small cottage with a very large deck that we live in. We tend to live on the deck year round as it is so beautiful and much warmer than the UK. We love to swim in the river. It is fun to wash our hair in the river too. We live only a quarter of a mile from the Layou River. We are lucky as we have no neighbours so it is very peaceful and quiet.

Dominica only has a small population, around 66,000 people. We also have the Carib Indians who are indigenous to Dominica. They live together on their own land rather like a reservation in the USA. The Carib Indians are great at making baskets and many crafts, which they sell to the tourists. They are also really good fishermen.

When I started writing to you I told you I am an artist. The project that I am doing at the moment is painting parrots and hummingbirds. We have copied the paintings onto mats and postcards, which we sell to the tourists and locals. The forestry commission here keep a very firm hand on our parrots as they were being killed and hunted and were becoming extinct. Laurie and I owned a parrot for many years and he died this year in June. I was so very, very sad that I started painting parrots to console myself and that is how the idea was born to do this for Dominica. So our parrot's spirit goes on as I have used Ernie a lot as the model and painted him the colour of the Sisserou and Jaco. The Sisserou parrot is known as the Imperial parrot and is bigger than the Jaco. The colour of the Sisserou is deep purplish blue and green, and the Jaco is green and red. They visit us here at our home at certain times of the year. They are fun to watch and are very noisy. They have plenty of fruit and nuts to live on. It is fantastic watching them in the wild.

Again I am so sorry this is late getting to you. Please keep in touch.

Best wishes,

Lisette & Laurie

Grenada

Kate works with turtles – which immediately makes her one of the coolest people ever in Toby's eyes! Through our research, Grenada is firmly embedded as the place in Toby's mind where he wants to go diving – both to see the turtles, and to discover the amazing underwater sculpture park.

Letter to Kate

Dear Kate,

How are you? Have you seen a turtle? How old do you have to be to join the volunteer project? What do the turtles eat? What do the children do in the club? What is your favourite species of turtle? We are going to like your Facebook page.

Bye,
Toby

Response from Kate

Dear Toby,

Thank you for your letter. I was really excited to receive your mail in my post box here in Grenada.

I am a marine biologist and specialize in working with sea turtles. I mostly work with the giant leatherback turtles, green turtles and hawksbill turtles.

Leatherback turtles are the biggest turtles on earth and have been living on earth for over a million years and have been in our oceans since dinosaurs were alive. A leatherback can grow

KENSINGTON PALACE

From: Miss Claudia Spens M.V.O.
          The Office of TRH The Duke and Duchess of Cambridge and HRH Prince Henry of Wales

Private and Confidential

9th October, 2015

Buckingham Palace

Toby wrote to the Duke and Duchess of Cambridge congratulating
them on the birth of Princess Charlotte and, although we'll keep
the response 'private and confidential', Toby was thrilled to receive a
letter of thanks.

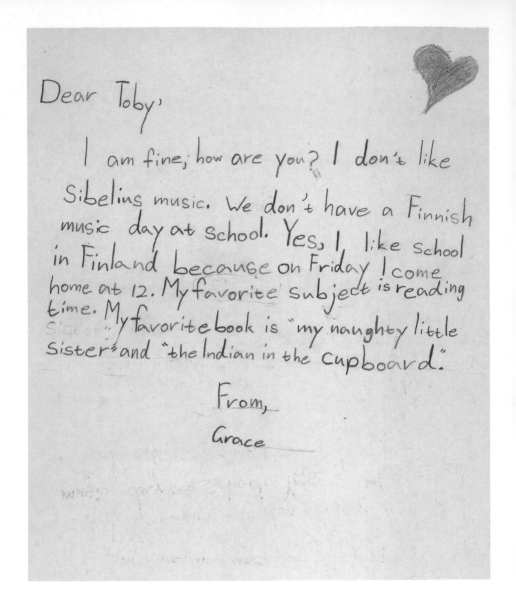

Dear Toby,

I am fine, how are you? I don't like Sibelius music. We don't have a Finnish music day at school. Yes, I, like school in Finland because on Friday I come home at 12. My favorite subject is reading time. My favorite book is "my naughty little Sister" and "the Indian in the Cupboard."

From,

Grace

Finland

Toby loved this very sweet letter and drawing
from a young Finnish girl called Grace.

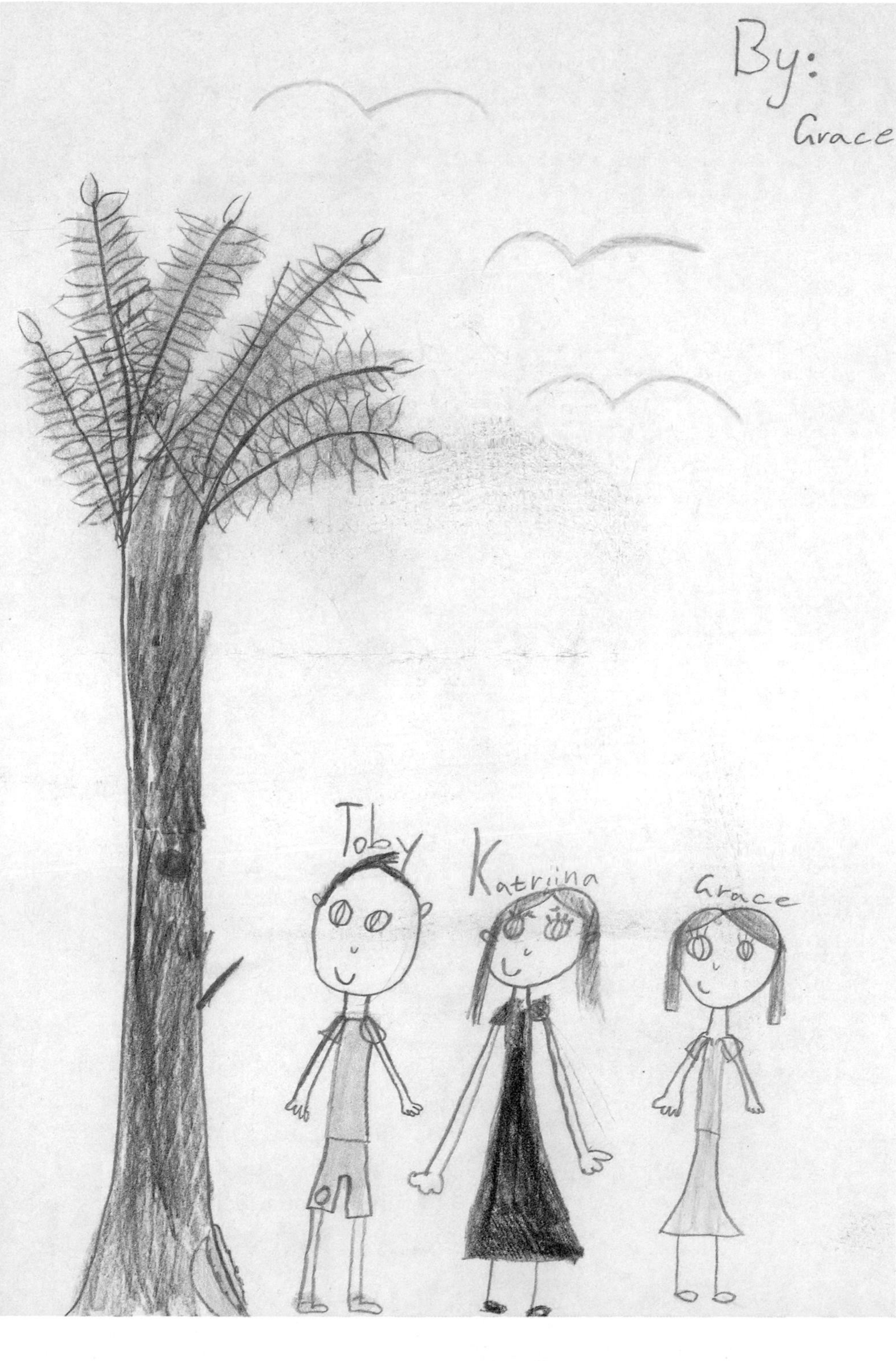
By:
Grace
Toby
Katriina
Grace

Dear Toby, A bumper letter from Lebanon

By Olivia Alabaster and
Nadia Massih
The Daily Star

BEIRUT: The way newspapers are made today is probably a lot less exciting than in the olden days, when journalists wrote on typewriters, news was spread around the world by telegram and the pages were laid out letter by letter in a printing press.

Today, we use the internet and our computers to do almost all of the work that goes into making the newspaper.

We use the internet to research stories, and to track down contacts who can provide the information and quotes for each article: much like how you and your mum used the internet to locate people to contact in every country around the world – a task I'm sure many journalists wouldn't be up to!

Once we have all the information we need, we write up the story, which begins with a "byline," the author's name. So yours would be "Toby Little." Then a "dateline," which is the city in which the story is written. Yours would be "Sheffield."

This helps the reader understand where the news is coming from, and who is writing it. If they had a query or a problem with the story, they could write to the newspaper and ask to be put in touch with that journalist.

We then try and tackle the essentials of the news story – what happened, who is involved, when and where it happened, and why it might have happened – if we know. Feature stories are generally longer than a typical news article, and they delve deeper into the issues involved: they are more like a short non-fiction story.

As our newspaper is based in Lebanon, The Daily Star focuses on local news, so we have reporters all around the country who send in stories to us, and we have reporters here in the Beirut office.

Some recent stories we have published have been about forest fires, people keeping lions as pets on city-center balconies, and Syrian refugee children living in Lebanon.

For international news, and news from other countries in the Middle East, we use something called a "wire agency," as we do not have our own reporters in each country. Each wire agency has their own staff all around the world. So we pay to subscribe to the wire agency, and they send us stories from their reporters that we can use in our newspaper.

As the reporters are writing, page designers are creating the layout of each page. They draw out a box for each article, and leave spaces for photos, headlines and adverts.

At the same time, our photographers are out taking pictures, and the photo editor is choosing the best photo to match each story.

After the reporters have written the story, they send it to the sub-editors.

The sub-editors read over the story to check that it makes sense and that all the spelling is correct.

They are reading the story as it looks on the page, so they make it fit perfectly in the box that the designers have drawn out. And they write headlines and picture captions to fit in the spaces provided.

There are also section editors working on each page, ensuring that all the news is covered and that journalists are meeting their deadlines.

Once each page is finished (our paper has 16 pages) it is taken to the editor of the paper, who is in charge of the whole operation. They read over it to make sure it all looks good and makes sense.

After that, each page is sent to the printers. Our final deadline is midnight. The printers work overnight to produce the paper, and then it is delivered across the country to newsagents in the early morning so that people can read the news over breakfast.

Lebanon

One of Toby's favourite letters ever! Venetia and her journalist colleagues at the *Daily Star* in Lebanon pulled out all the stops and created a front page just for Toby using his questions as hooks for articles.

Bosnia & Herzegovina

Every child at this school drew Toby a picture about one aspect of their life – food, landscape or musical instruments – so that together, they are like a little patchwork of life in Bosnia & Herzegovina.

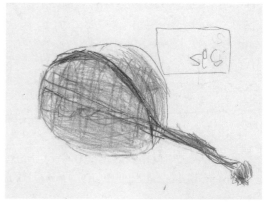

Sultanate of Oman
Green Turtle

Hello Toby! Thank you for your wonderful letter, and for the postcard. You must have tired fingers from all that writing! To answer your questions; I haven't been to Jalali fort because it is closed to the public, but I have visited lots of other amazing forts here. I think Nakhal fort is my favourite so far.

I haven't met the Sultan yet, but maybe one day! As for the sultanas, the name comes from the grape that is used to make sultanas. The grape comes from Turkey, and was named after the wife of the Sultan in Turkey, who was called the Sultana. They use lots of sultanas in the food here, it is delicious! Oman also has lots of turtles, so here is a picture of a turtle making a nest. Take care and good luck! Jeanne

Oman

Toby received this fascinating response from Jeanne to his question:
'Are sultanas called sultanas because they are for the sultan?'

Iran

Most children around the world are fascinated by myths and monsters, so after receiving Kareh's wonderful picture, Toby sat down to learn more about the terrifying Iranian 'Simorgh'.

Writing to the World

Dear Kareh, how are you?
How do you spell Toby in Persian?
Are you spelling tests hard in school?
Have you been up Tehran Tower?
What is your favourite mythical creature?
Mine is the thunderbird, or maybe Pegasus but I don't know every mythical creature.
What is your school like?
Do you learn english?
Bye Toby

I drew you a yeti

My favourite mythical creature is Simorgh
سیمرغ

I'm learning english

1*
Toby would you like to visit Tehran some day? Please come to visit me. I am learning English. By then hopefully we can talk

١* اورژ گلی تو نمی خواهی یه بار بیای تهران؟ من مشغول انگلیسی یادگرفتن هستم. خوب شده و من می توانم با تو حرف بزنم.

Canada

When Toby researched Canadian myths, he came across the Ogopogo, a monster that supposedly lives in a lake in British Columbia – a bit like the Loch Ness Monster in Scotland.

Michigan

Melissa from the Henry Ford Museum in Michigan invited Toby to visit, and eighteen months later he was able to do just that! Here he is sitting on the famous 'Rosa Parks Bus'.

taller than an adult man, weigh more than a piano and they eat their body weight in jellyfish every day!

I have seen lots of turtles this year and my team has recorded over 1,000 turtle sightings and over 800 nests so far; our biggest turtle had a shell length of 171cm. Turtle eggs take around 65 days to incubate before hatching. We are seeing lots of baby turtles scurrying down the beach into the ocean at the moment.

In our local primary school we have an environmental science club where each week our students learn about turtles, reefs, oceans, climate change and the environment. Tomorrow we are learning about coral reefs and what creatures live there.

My favourite turtles are green turtles because they have a very pretty shell and you can snorkel with them in the water. Have you seen a turtle on your travels yet? They are incredible creatures to watch on the beach and in the ocean.

Grenada is known as the spice isle and lots of different spices are grown here, like cinnamon, nutmeg, cocoa, sugar cane and cloves. We make our own chocolate bars on the island. They are very yummy! Please find yours enclosed to enjoy ☺

Good luck with all your letter writing and look forward to seeing you on your Facebook page.

Kindest regards,

Kate

Project Manager

Ocean Spirits

Guatemala

Toby wrote to Trish early on in the project, when he still assumed that every volcano by default must be a bubbling, lava-spewing dangerous place. He grew very concerned for Trish's safety, so he was happy when her letter reassured him.

Letter to Trish

Hi Trish,
How are you? Have you ever been on a boat on Atitlán Lake? Are you scared living near San Pedro volcano?
  Adios,
  Toby

Response from Trish

Hi Toby,
I am very well. Thank you for letting me participate in your project. My husband and I often take boats across the lake. We often take a boat to a town called Tzununa, where there is a beautiful water-fall. Don't worry about the volcano. It is not one of the active ones luckily for us.
  Trish

United States of America

Melissa got in touch with us after Toby's project went viral – she works at the Henry Ford Museum in Michigan, and noticed Toby's interest in the Rosa Parks Bus. When Toby wrote to her, she sent the most wonderful and detailed response. She suggested that Toby should come and see the museum for himself – and, nearly eighteen months later, luck would have it that we were able to do just that! So Melissa is the only person Toby exchanged letters with whom we actually met in person. She generously spent nearly a whole day showing us around the museum, and we can confirm that she is just as wonderful in person as her letter suggested – and Toby got to sit on the Rosa Parks Bus too!

Letter to Melissa

Dear Melissa,

How are you? Have you sat in the Rosa Parks Bus? I really, really want to! What is your favourite exhibit at the Henry Ford Museum? What food do you eat?

Bye,

Toby

Response from Melissa

Hello Toby,

How are you doing? How is school going? What are you learning? Have you learned anything cool or neat in history?

Wow, your letter came to me when I really needed it the most. I have been extremely busy the last couple of weeks at work and was opening my mail when your letter popped up. It was great to hear from you and I hope you do not mind but I shared it with a couple dozen co-workers and friends. I have told everyone about your project, and in talking about it everyone gets excited that you at your age are so very ambitious. One good friend, her name is Lynn, said that you must have an old soul to enjoy things that most kids your age could care less about. Now, let's get to the major questions in your letter and then some history fun for you.

Question 1: How am I?

I am doing really well. I just finished several really long work weeks. I am taking a small break now.

Question 2: Have I ever sat on the Rosa Parks Bus?

Yes, I have several times. I have sat in different seats on the bus, as well as in the seat that she refused to give up. I will also say that I have presented Rosa's story to visitors that have come to the museum as well. It is a great story and one that, through a recording, Rosa tells herself. If you make it to Michigan, I will be your personal tour guide in both the museum and the village, so that you may sit on the Rosa Parks Bus.

Question 3: What is my favorite exhibit at the Henry Ford Museum?

Wow, Toby!! Try to ask a difficult question!! Let's see, I have to say that I enjoy all of the Henry Ford, however I mostly walk and enjoy the Henry Ford Museum and Greenfield Village.

Now, I have to tell you that my favorites change because I am pretty much always finding something new and exciting, and therefore my favorites change.

In the museum right now I have to say that I like the Allegheny, the Bugatti Royale, the Wienermobile, and the Liberty and Justice for All exhibits. I find that I enjoy the Allegheny locomotive because of the size and to know that when they brought that to the museum it came in on its own power. I enjoy the Bugatti, because it is the most expensive car in the world; there are only a few still around and I have had the pleasure to see it be driven around the village during one of the car shows that the Henry Ford has during the summer. It is an extremely beautiful car and one of many unique cars that is in the collection. The Wienermobile is just a standout type of artefact that the museum has and one that brings a smile to pretty much anyone's face. Now, the best exhibit and the one probably you and I would most enjoy is the Liberty and Justice for All exhibit. This exhibit tells the story of my nation from the Revolution to Civil Rights. This is where the Rosa Parks Bus is, in addition to the Lincoln Chair and one of Washington's camp sets.

In Greenfield Village, which is part of the entire

complex, I like the running steam-engine trains, Thomas Edison's Menlo Park Laboratory, and Main Street district, which has the Wright Brothers' home and cycle shop. My favorite train engine happens to be the Baldwin No. 7, which took 7 years because Thomas Edison was actually a part of everything and even recreated his light bulb experiment after the move when the village opened in October of 1929. The Main Street District is cool for its different aspects of daily life. In the district, there is the Logan County Courthouse where Abraham Lincoln practiced law in his early life, and the building holds a corner chest that Abraham and his father built together. The Wright Brothers' home and cycle shop is where they created the first successful flying airplane.

Question 4: What food do you eat?

All kinds of food, but when you work where I do you get to try out some old recipes. At Greenfield Village they make a really good beef stew and during the holidays they have fresh carved roast beef sandwiches that are amazing. In Dearborn we have a lot of Arabic food to choose from as well as other nationalities. I really don't miss meals with all the great food that we have here.

Today, here are some Michigan facts that I thought you might like.

1) Any Michigander can tell you where they live by holding up their hand and pointing.
2) A Michigan saying: 'If you don't like the weather, wait five minutes – it will change.'
3) Michigan has the longest freshwater coastline in the US and the second largest coastline in the US next to Alaska.
4) Michigan is the only state in the US north of Canada. South-western Ontario (Windsor) is south of Detroit.
5) The Upper Peninsula is mostly forested.
6) The people of the Upper Peninsula are called Yoopers and they call anyone living in the mitten (Lower Peninsula) 'trolls' because they live under the bridge (the Mackinac Bridge).

Last, before I close my letter to you, Toby, I just want to wish you a happy birthday and a safe holiday season.

Until next time,

Melissa

PS Look for a package and have Mummy let me know when you receive it.

SOUTH AMERICA

Argentina

Patricia was our first South American contact;
it was so exciting when her letter came back! Sabine
has been to Argentina, so we also had some
photos to look at as we researched the letter.

Letter to Patricia

Hi Patricia,
How are you? We looked at pictures of Argentina –
why are the houses in La Boca lots of colours? Have
you been to Iguazú Waterfalls?
   Bye,
   Toby

Response from Patricia

Hi Toby,
How are you? I'm very happy because your letter
has finally arrived.

   I live in Buenos Aires city, the capital city of
Argentina. You asked me about La Boca; well,
there is a lot to say about La Boca.

   There is no other neighbourhood in my city with
such vibrant colours. The soccer club stadium that
bears the same name and is the passion of many
Argentines is a few blocks from the river (Ria-
chuelo). La Boca was born as a result of the influx
of immigrants from different origins that arrived by
sea to the port of Buenos Aires.

One of its mythical streets is Caminito (Little Path), a no-exit road with a strong tango feel. A very famous painter called Benito Quinquela Martin gave this road its name. This artist's works are famous because they show the image of La Boca workers in the early 20th century.

I haven't been to Iguazu Falls yet. My sister-in-law went there last month and she said it's a wonderful place. The name 'Iguazu' comes from the Guarani or Tupi words *y* meaning 'water' and *uasu* meaning 'big'. Did you know Iguazu Falls is one of the new Seven Wonders of Nature?

I visited England a long time ago, though I didn't go to your city . . .

Thanks for your lovely letter. If you want to know more about Argentina, just let me know.

Love,

Patricia

Brazil

We have to apologize to Luna, because, as far as we know, she was the only contact we ever forgot about! It is sometimes a bit tricky to remember whose addresses we have, and Luna got in touch at a time when we had lots of Brazilian addresses. We found her address a couple of months later and emailed her to apologize. Thankfully she was still happy to be Toby's contact! Researching Luna's letter made us dance through the living room to the music of Adoniran Barbosa, and we love the idea of having fruit fests all year round!

Letter to Luna

Dear Luna,

How are you? Are you named after Luna Lovegood? What is your favourite place in São Paulo? What is your job? What is the Fig Fest about? Have you been? Do you listen to Adoniran Barbosa? I like him.

    Bye,
    Toby

Response from Luna

Hi Toby!

How are you? I am so happy to be one of your many writing partners around the world!

    I was not named after Luna Lovegood. I was born a few years before the Harry Potter books were written. I started reading the first book when I was 10 years old, and the last book was released only when I was in college! Luna is not a very common name in Brazil – it means 'moon' in Spanish and Italian. 'Moon' in Portuguese is *lua*.

    I think my favourite place in São Paulo is

Ibirapuera Park. Have you seen pictures of it? It is a very big park right in the middle of the city, kind of like Central Park in NYC. *Ibirapuera* means something like 'fallen tree' in Tupi-Guarani, that is the language the native people spoke before the Portuguese came to Brazil. There are many places with Tupi-Guarani names here, but people don't usually know their meaning.

I am a pharmacist and I work with cosmetics. I develop sunscreen and make-up formulas. I really like it because it is very dynamic, plus I get to travel a lot to conferences and trade shows – and I love to travel! I have a sticker map above my bed where I pin all the places I have visited. I also collect postcards from places I have been and I always ask my friends to send them to me from wherever they go to.

The Fig Fest is part of the 'Fruit Circuit'. There are 10 towns that participate, and each one is famous for the production of one specific fruit. Valinhos is the fig town! So every January we have the Fig Fest, where you can buy all kinds of fig products, like jam, juice, candy. There is also music, playgrounds for kids and all kinds of food. If you go around the other towns you will find the Grape

Fest, the Guava Fest, the Strawberry Fest, and so on. Fruit fests all year long! I have been to the Fig Fest and the Grape Fest a few times, but I missed them both this year. Maybe I'll be there next year, then I can send you a picture!

I am glad you like Adoniran Barbosa. He was a great singer and songwriter. Everyone in Brazil can sing at least one of his songs. I am sure you will also like Demônios da Garoa. They were a samba group that recorded many songs written by Adoniran Barbosa. I believe '*Trem das Onze*' is the most famous.

I hope you have the chance to visit Brazil someday!
Love from Brazil,
Luna ☺

Chile

Quite a few people have told us that Toby's letters have encouraged them to go out and explore a part of their country or city they hadn't yet been to, and Toby loves the idea that his project is helping other people to go exploring, too.

Letter to Patricia

Dear Patricia,
How are you? Have you seen the blue whale skeleton at the Natural History Museum? Please could you send us a recipe from Chile? Do you go skiing? Are you scared of earthquakes?
    Bye,
    Toby

Response from Patricia

Dear Toby,
First of all, I would like to say that I'm so sorry for taking so long to reply.
    Thanks to you, I went to the Museum of Natural History for the first time!! And I found the whale you mentioned!!
    I've never been to skiing, because I live in the city, but I promise as soon as I go there, I'll send you pictures.
    About the earthquakes, I don't actually fear them, but I do respect them a lot.

I'd like to keep writing to you and maybe next time I could send some Chilean vocabulary!!

I'd like to know what kind of music, sports, or TV show do you like. Do you have sisters and brothers? Be nice, kind and help your parents as much as you can.

I hope you can write back asap. Bye!!

Patricia

Peru

We are always especially grateful to those early contacts of Toby's who went out of their way to tell us more than he asked about – in the early days writing just a couple of questions would take him a very long time! Percy answered all of Toby's questions very carefully, and sent lots of pictures and additional information. Toby often asks about earthquakes, partly because he has never experienced one, and partly because he is interested in how they happen. The project made us look at tectonic plates and explore why some places have more earthquakes than others.

Letter to Percy

Hi Percy,

How are you? Were you there for the earthquake in 2005? Have you ever swum with dolphins? What is your job?

Bye,
Toby

Response from Percy

Hi Toby!

I give you my most sincere congratulations, for your project. Thanks for including me and letting me be a small part of it.

About your question, there was an earthquake in Peru on September 25, 2005, in magnitude 7.5 on the Richter scale. Fortunately, I was 476km west of there, in Piura. I remember sitting at my computer writing on the third floor, when around 9:00 p.m. I felt a little shake, nothing to worry about. In my area the earthquake was rated with an intensity of 3 with weak shaking and no material damage. The next day we received the news on TV about the towns most affected, subsequently reaching an estimated 39,000 people homeless in 7 regions in Peru. This earthquake was also felt in Brazil, Ecuador and Colombia. I am attaching some graphics for more information.

About the dolphins, I will say that I have only seen them swimming in the open sea. Here in Peru there are two dolphins in captivity as I read. They arrived to Peru in 1997 at the ages of 5 and 9 years old, but now the place to go to visit is closed to the public and I don't know why. It says they're fine and they eat 25kg of fish a day. I read that you could go swimming with them, learn to communicate with them by signs and also feed them. It would be a good option to try someday.

I am an industrial engineer. My profession allows me to develop in various fields, which involve administration, security, design and resource optimization. It is general knowledge production. I can work in hospitals, supermarkets, airports, hotels, warehouses, factories, etc. I am currently working on logistics for an oil company. What I do is make contact with several companies to offer me a certain product or service that we need, then each company sends me a price. Of those prices, I calculate one.

The same one is published on the Internet in order to compete nationally or internationally for having a sales or service contract with us.

Did you know that you can know something of our culture in the UK? Peru has a very strong food culture, and it is becoming known in different parts of the world. You can go to Tito's Peruvian Restaurant, to Coya Restaurant or Lima. The last one is close to a street in London that bears my name. Nice! ☺

I wish you luck with your project, Toby. Say hi to your mom!

Percy

Uruguay

Maria is a glass artist in Uruguay, but she is also a trained biologist and so could tell us all about fossils in Uruguay. Toby never gets tired of asking about fossils!

Letter to Maria

Dear Maria,

How are you? Are you still a biologist? Do you know anything about fossils in Uruguay? What do you make out of glass? Do you go to the carnival?

Bye,
Toby

Response from Maria

Dear Toby,

How are you? I was very happy to get your letter; I can see that you have a very nice handwriting! You know a very close friend of mine lived in Sheffield? What a coincidence!

Yes, I am a biologist and I work in a laboratory. Here in Uruguay in 2001 fossils were found! They are 250 million years old and are from a species called *Pelycosauriae*, which is very, very rare and were only found in Russia [before this].

I am also an artist. I work with glass. I have an oven where I put the glass and it melts at very high temperatures – this way I can make it take the form I like – I also write on the glass messages for the people to read.

I hope you have a lot of good friends and that you like to play a lot. I like it too! Specially outdoors! I send you a big hug from Uruguay!

Kisses,

Maria

AFRICA

Algeria

We got to know Cari and her family via Facebook, and Cari told us that her nine-year-old daughter Aishah would be happy to be Toby's writing partner in Algeria. Toby thought it was amazing that Aishah was learning three languages (Arabic, French and English).

Letter to Cari and family

Dear everybody,
How are you? Have you been to the Djémila ruins?
Have you seen a fennec fox? What food do you
eat?
    Bye,
    Toby

Response from Cari

Dear Toby,
We live in Setif, Algeria. Our town was named
Setifis by the Romans and it has kept that name
pretty much. We have five children: Aishah (9),
Abdullah (6), Zoulaikha (4), Khadidja (2) and
Youcef (1).

    Aishah is your penpal. I am writing for her
because she speaks Arabic, French and English, but
is just learning to write English. Aishah says: We
have seen the fennek foxes in the zoo. They are so
cute with black eyes and golden fur. They live in the
Sahara Desert, about 3 hours from us.

    We have been to Djémila. It is so cool. You can

still walk through the city. Their library and houses were very small. The prison is only the size of a tiny closet and it is mostly underground. Yuck!

We eat lots of stews here over grain called cous-cous. Also we love cakes and cookies made with nuts, honey and powdered sugar.

Kids here are just the same I think. I am on the swim team and love to play with friends ☺

Aishah Mokrani (9)

Benin

Simon and Benjamin's letter was accompanied
by a card saying 'It is never far to a friend's house';
it seemed the perfect note to sum up Toby's project.
Plus, Toby found out that children love
collecting fossils all over the world!

Letter to Simon and Benjamin

Hi Simon and Benjy,
How are you? Do you go to school? What food do
you eat? What is life like in Benin? Do you speak
Fon?
   Bye,
   Toby

Response from Simon and Benjamin

Dear Toby,
School is nice, because Papa teaches us in French.
We eat pounded yams. Lots of people here are
farmers. They grow corn and cotton.
   In Benin there are more than 50 languages.
Where we live they speak Monkole and we speak it
a bit. We like our house. Simon is also interested in
fossils and likes trying to find some in our
compound.
   Bye,
   Simon and Benjamin

Burkina Faso

Stephanie's letter had lots and lots of information, and her style of writing made us feel like we were in Burkina Faso with her! In England people say 'Hi, how are you?', and people joke that you would never say 'Actually, I'm not very well', but the greetings Stephanie describes in her letter sound very complex and tricky; we wouldn't want to get them wrong and offend anybody! It also made Toby glad that he got a meal at school every day.

Letter to Stephanie

Dear Stephanie,
How are you? What work do you do in Burkina
Faso? Why are you volunteering? Do the children
go to school? What do you eat?
    Bye,
    Toby

Response from Stephanie

Hello Toby,
Nice to hear from you! Your project sounds very
interesting and cool. Thank you very much for
making me a part of it! Burkina Faso is a country
that very few people have heard of – so it is my
pleasure to tell you a little more about it.

    Burkina is a small and very poor country in West
Africa – and it is very, very hot here. Most of the
country is just desert and sand, but I live in the
south so there are a few trees, which is nice.

    I work on public health projects here, which
means I try to prevent people from getting sick, and
help those that are already sick. Stopping a sickness

called malaria is one of my main tasks. Have you heard of malaria before? It doesn't exist any more in the UK or Europe, but in countries like Burkina Faso, in most parts of Africa and Asia, malaria has been responsible for many deaths – unfortunately.

It's spread by mosquitos but people here don't seem to understand that very well. In my village for instance, where we speak Dagara, the word for malaria literally translates as 'sickness of the cold'. So basically my job is to teach people about health topics so that they can stay strong and healthy.

Only some kids go to school here, as families often do not have enough money to pay the small school fee. If that is the case, it is generally the boys who are sent, while the girls stay home to do house-hold chores. There is also only one primary school in my village, so if the children do get to go to school it isn't for very long. The nearest middle school is about 15km away, and the high school is 25km away. This is the case in most areas and unfortunately that is why very, very few people in Burkina Faso can read and write. Only 27% of the population!

I often work at the school, and really enjoy it. I just started a school garden there, so that lunches could be served to the students and they wouldn't have to go all day without eating. Before the garden, most of the kids had to wait till they got back home at night-time to eat – although sometimes I saw the boys shoot lizards and birds with their sling-shots to cook up for lunch. I hope that having a nutritious meal will help the kids stay in school; I don't know how they can concentrate with empty bellies.

Most people in Burkina Faso eat something called *tô* every day. It's just made out of corn flour and is cooked into a jello-like consistency. You take a handful of jello (because we only eat with our hands here) and dip it into a sauce, which varies depending on the season. Unfortunately there aren't many vitamins in *tô*, and there are many times when families cannot afford to make a sauce with it – so many people are malnourished.

Although it is very, very poor, Burkina Faso is full of lovely and hospitable people. Very few visitors have come to Burkina Faso, so most places I go have never seen any white people, but I am always welcomed with open arms. It is very important to say hello to people here, and each greeting is quite lengthy. You not only say hello, but you have to ask many things like 'How did you sleep? How is your family? How is work? How is your health? The kids' health? Is there peace?' or else it is considered rude. It is kind of tiring sometimes. Haha.

There aren't any cool animals here that you would normally think of when you think of Africa. Mostly just farm animals like donkeys, goats, sheep, chickens and pigs. There are some elephants out in the east but I haven't seen any of them yet. I actually just got a baby goat as a pet. I am very excited about it. Here, having farm animals is how people show wealth, and since I didn't have any animals my village chief gave me a goat so that I wouldn't be disrespected in the community. That was nice.

People are very traditional here, and there are many strange sacrifices and ceremonies that I still don't understand. Like at funerals, for instance, they sit the dead body in an open field, and then the guests have to dance around it and throw money at it when they are done. The first time I participated in a funeral I was very shocked and afraid, but now I've done it so many times that it all seems normal!

I've been working in Burkina Faso for well over a year now, and feel very lucky for having this opportunity! Although sometimes it is hard. I've grown used to living without electricity, running water and cold drinks among other things. I can honestly say that I am very happy here, far away from the comfort of home.

I hope this letter has helped you learn a little about Burkina Faso – please let me know if you have any questions! Good luck with the end of your project, and keep up this curious mind of yours – it's very impressive!

Best wishes,
Stephanie

Chad

This letter contained one of the loveliest surprises ever. When Lorna responded, she not only answered all of Toby's questions, but she also told us that they had named one of the local wild elephants after Toby. Toby thought that was incredibly cool!

Letter to Lorna and Rhian

Hi Lorna and Rhian,
How are you? What do you use the plane for in the park? Where do you go to get your food? What does a scout do?
    Bye,
    Toby

Response from Rhian and Lorna

Dear Toby,
Thank you very much for your letter. And well done to you for doing this big project. It is a very good idea.

    The picture above is of some wild elephants that often come to our house to drink water. They even drink from our hosepipe if we hold it for them! The smallest elephant in the middle has been named Toby after you.

    We use the plane in the park for doing anti-poaching patrols. In a park where animals are being protected we have to stop bad people from coming in to kill the animals – in the case of the elephants

138

they do it for the tusks, also called ivory. Some animals are killed for the meat, others for their skins. It is our job as conservationists to stop the poachers from killing wild animals. So the plane does flights along the park boundary, around the elephant herd and around the other animals – to always look for signs of bad people.

We also use the plane to supply places in the park where we cannot drive. We have 11 small bush airstrips that we use. Here is a picture of the plane on one of the bush strips with some of the game scouts. This plane is a Cessna 180 – this is a very good plane for flying into short, uneven air-strips – it is known as a good 'bush plane' – we even land her where there is no airstrip! We have big wheels on her, which helps her land on rough ground. The park manager of Zakouma is the pilot of this plane.

The game scouts, as in this picture, are the people who do patrols in the park, always on the look-out for poachers or signs of activity in the park that is not allowed. They do their patrols on foot, on horses, on bicycles and on motorbikes. They spend 7 days in the bush at a time in teams of 6 men and cover big distances each day while on patrol. They are very important people and we cannot protect the wildlife without them.

We buy our food in two places – either in Am Timan, which is a small town about 1 and a half hours' drive from our home. This town does not have very much in the shops so we also buy our food in the capital of Chad, the city of N'Djamena. This city is not very big and we can also not buy everything we need there. But we can get enough food here to be able to eat well. They say that now N'Djamena is the most expensive city in the world! Imagine that! We eat very basic food: lots of rice and vegetables. We get lovely mangoes and water-melons in Chad so we eat a lot of that. We only go to the shops about 2 or 3 times a month so we keep a lot of food in the freezer and the pantry.

I hope that this has answered your questions, Toby, and that you enjoy the photographs. I end this letter with a photograph of my husband, the park manager, watering an elephant at our house! We have lived in the bush in Africa for over 30 years and have never had wild elephants do this before! Rather special, isn't it?

With lots of love,

Rhian and Lorna

Liberia

Toby was impressed with how official Francis's letter sounded. Francis works for the Liberian government, which is why Toby wondered about the president. It is difficult to understand that they are actually real people!

Letter to Francis

Dear Francis,
How are you? Have you met President Sirleaf?
What food do you eat? Have you been to the
jungle?
  Bye,
  Toby

Response from Francis

Responses to Questionnaires
My Dearest Toby Little:
I am great. I blessed God for good and sound
health and I hope you are also doing well in
health.

  Before responding to your questions let me firstly
commend you for such a meaningful initiative and
also hail your mom for standing by you in fulfilling
your dream.

Question #1: Have you met President Sirleaf?
  Yes, but not personally. I met President Ellen
Johnson Sirleaf in 2008 at the launch of the

County Development Steering Committee in Bopolu, Gbarpolu County. As president of the Gbarpolu University Student Association at the African Methodist Episcopal University (AMEU), I led a group of students at the launch of County Development Steering Committee in Bopolu, Gbarpolu County, where we called on the president through a petition to make human source development a priority issue amongst many developmental issues in the county.

However, in answering your question as to whether I have met President Sirleaf, again I can safely say yes; I have met President Sirleaf but my coming into contact with her was at a national platform and not a personal interface.

Question #2: What food do you eat?

In Liberia, rice is consumed much more than any other food. In fact, it is eaten at least twice a day. Foreign rice, or *posava* (as it is locally called), is considered much better than locally grown rice because of the rocks that get mixed up with the local rice during harvesting. Palm oil or palm butter (soup made from palm nut) usually comes with the meal, and wine is also made from the palm nut. Cassava leaves and potato leaves are both boiled and eaten like spinach. Sugar cane is either refined or, after cutting through the tough bark, the sweet juice is sucked straight out of the cane bought at the marketplace. Fufu (a doughy food that accompanies most meals) can be made from fermented rice, plantain, cassava, corn or yam. The starchy food is dried, pounded until ground, boiled and rolled into two-inch ovals. Cassava is the second staple food after rice in Liberia. It is used to make fufu; a variation called dumboy is boiled before mashing. Fufu is swallowed instead of chewed. It is popularly eaten with a spicy soup.

This is just to mention a few. To directly answer your question, I eat rice every day and once in a while it is accompanied with fufu. I come from the Belle ethnicity in western Liberia; all of the social ethnic groups in this region are more used to eating only rice as compared to other regions that always have fufu accompanying their food (rice).

Question #3: Have you been to the jungle?

No, Toby Little, I have not been to the jungle but I have been to the forest. While under 12 years of age, I was often taken to the forest to hunt and to farm by my senior brothers in Gbarpolu County, western Liberia.

It is my hope that these responses will make some impact to your project.

Regards,

Sincerely yours,

Francis

Liberia Contact for Little Boy Writing to the World

Libya

Hassan went to a lot of trouble for Toby: sending a map, a flag pin, some stamps and lots of photos in answer to Toby's questions. We would love to go and see the rock art in the Sahara Desert!

Letter to Hassan

Hi Hassan,
How are you? Have you seen the rock art from the Sahara Desert? What food do you eat in Libya?
    Bye,
    Toby

Response from Hassan

To my friend Toby,
I am very well, thank you. I was so pleased when I got your letter. You have very nice handwriting. I hope mine will be as nice one day. I'm 19 years old and hoping to become a journalist. So thank you for giving me a chance to practise on my writing skills ☺

    I'm from a town called Towcara, in the east of the country. In the map I have given you, you can see where it is. It is a lovely place and is famous for having very old buildings. They were built a very, very long time ago.

    As for your question, yes, I have seen the rock art in the Sahara Desert. And they are amazing.

Other places you may have heard of are the great Ubari lakes. These amazing lakes are in the Ubari Desert. There are 4 lakes. One of them named Qabar Ouu is so salty you float, even without moving. So it's great fun. The desert is very cool. It is very big and at night you can't see anything except the stars and the moon. Now I love animals and one animal that is known also as the Ship of the Desert is the camel. Did you know the people who look after the camels have to walk them right across the desert? Sometimes they go 3 months without seeing another person.

As for the food, well, we Libyans love food ☺ One of my favourite is called aseeda. It's very much like porridge, but just a bit thicker. And the best thing about it is you have to eat it with your hands. Which is great fun. We also have bazeen, roshda, couscous and osban.

I have put some pictures of everything I told you about, with little notes written on the back.

I hope you like your Libya flag pin and hope one day you will come and visit Libya and we can take you to see all of the great things you can find in Libya.

I hope this has answered your questions about Libya. It was very nice to hear from you. Thank you for writing.

Your new Libyan friend,

Hassan

Madagascar

Madagascar is one of Toby's favourite countries, and one he is desperate to visit. Guno's letter reached us in a rather complicated way, via Sarah, who works in Guno's village and facilitated the exchange. The letter was first sent to Sarah's mum, who forwarded it to us, and also added a letter of her own. Toby was fascinated to learn that Guno's name has different spellings because people in his village don't usually write things down!

Letter to Guno

Hi Guno,
How are you? Do you still go to school or do you work? What wild animals are living near you? What do you eat?
  Bye,
  Toby

Response from Guno

Hi Toby,
How are you? My name is Guno. I'm 17 years old. I live in Manafiafy.
  My job is weighing lobsters and fish. Before I was a student but now I'm not a student. I studied with ONG Azafady English in Manafiafy.
  The animals living near me are braine lemur, mouse lemur, woolly lemur and two fat-tail dwarf lemurs. Also cameleons, snakes. These animals are living next to my village.
  My birthday is in Novembre. I was born in 1996.
  I like music. Akon and Micheal Jacson my favourites.

Thank you very much.
Bye,
Guno

*

Response from Sarah's mum

Dear Toby,

My grown-up daughter, Sarah, is working in Madagascar teaching people to embroider things that they can sell to help feed their families.

She has made many friends in the village. One of them is Guno, who plays a Manafiafy guitar and Sarah plays the drums. I have sent a picture of Guno that I have printed from Sarah's video. Guno asked Sarah to bring this letter for you as there is nowhere in Sainte Luce for him to post it. You can find out more about where Guno lives by looking at the Azafady website and Facebook pages, and you can see more of Sarah's pictures of Sainte Luce on the Stitch Sainte Luce website, although it is out of date now as Sarah has been in Madagascar for more than a year. There is a picture of Sarah on the Azafady web page for their Madagascar staff, and some pictures of the embroidery on the Azafady shop page.

I didn't know anything about you Writing to the World until Guno's letter came to my house with Sarah's letter. It's a very interesting project.

By the way, sometimes Guno's name is spelt 'Juno' and sometimes 'Guno'. Most people in the village of Manafiafy don't need to write, so most only write their names, but Guno went to school in the village and learned some English. Sarah says his name is 'Gino' so I think that's how he says it. He speaks Malagasy, but it is said 'Malagash'! Guno helps Sarah around the house and now has a proper job weighing fish when the fishermen get back. If they get lobsters, they sell them and they are sent to Antananarivo, which is why they have to be weighed.

Sarah loves living in Manafiafy and is working there until July next year. Sometimes she Skypes me when she is in Fort Dauphin and tells me about the village. Next time I talk to her I will tell her more about you Writing to the World and let her know that your letter from Guno has been posted with the picture she asked me to print for you.

I hope you don't mind me writing to you but I

Currently, about 750 languages are spoken in India and 86 scripts are being used. In Delhi, Hindi is most commonly spoken.

This is your name in Hindi:

टोबी लिटल

(Toby) (Little)

Here are some more Hindi words and phrases:

- Namaste (Hello)
(नमस्ते)
- Dhanyavaad (Thank You)
(धन्यवाद)

- Aap kaise hain?
(आप कैसे हैं?)
(How are you?)

- Main theek hoon.
(मैं ठीक हूँ)
(I'm fine.)

chumbak

India

One of Toby's letters went to Tanya in New Delhi. She sent us lots and lots of information, including a letter decorated with a traditional Indian block print (over the page).

Dear Toby,

I hope this letter finds you in good health. I really admire your project "Writing to the World". You have done an amazing job!

I live in New Delhi but sadly I have been to the Lotus Temple only once, and that too a long time ago! The Taj Mahal is in Agra which is 3 hours away from Delhi and I have visited it only once as well. It is very, very beautiful. Maybe one day, you can visit India and see it yourself!

Since I am in college, I have to spend most of my day running; to classes or to catch a metro train ~~and~~ home. As a result, I mostly wear jeans or an Indian costume called a salwar kameez. But I wore a sari for my cousin's wedding!

All the best for the rest of your project and take care!

Bye! -Tanya.

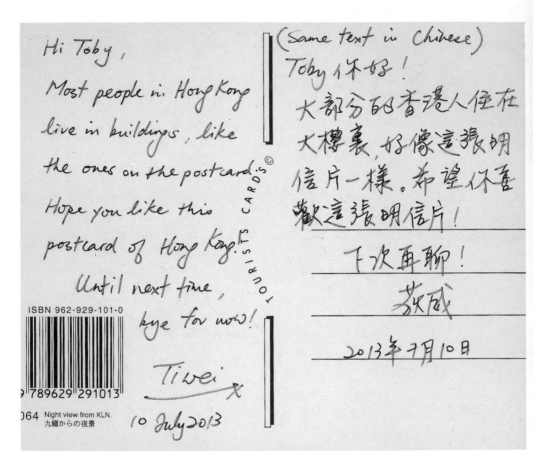

Hi Toby,
Most people in Hong Kong
live in buildings, like
the ones on the postcard.
Hope you like this
postcard of Hong Kong.
Until next time,
bye for now!
Tiwei x
10 July 2013

ISBN 962-929-101-0
9 789629 291013
064 Night view from KLN.
九龍からの夜景

TOURISTS CARD.S©

(Same text in Chinese)
Toby 你好!
大部分的香港人住在
大樓裏,好像這張明
信片一樣。希望你喜
歡這張明信片!
下次再聊!
荻威
2013年7月10日

Hong Kong

Tiwei's postcard sparked Toby's fascination with the Mandarin language and it continues to this day. He is desperate to visit China so that he can practice what he's learnt!

Dearest Toby,

Thank you for your letter. How do you do? I am fine.

The Botanic Gardens is beautiful. I celebrated my birthday this year by having a picnic at the Gardens. I enjoy attending concerts and plays at the Esplanade. Every Saturday morning, I go to the beach for a jog with my sister.

School was fun and I certainly miss my schooling days. The crescent moon on our flag represents a rising young nation — we are very proud to turn 50 years old this year!

Loves
Bing.

Singapore
This was one of the most beautiful letters Toby received – we loved the watercolour paper!

Australia

Toby loved that all the children at this school in Sydney drew pictures of whatever they liked most about where they lived, and whatever they wanted to share with Toby: the Sydney Opera House, the Harbour Bridge, lorikeets, and kangaroos.

Dear Toby

a kangaroo

Love George

Dear Toby

I am 5

Rainbow
Rambo
Lorikeet
Lorykee

I Liv
in hantishil.

Lov saskia

New Zealand

The project started with a book called *A Letter to New Zealand*, so the country has an important place in our hearts. Toby's contact there was four-year-old Eloise, who responded with a drawing of an exploding rainbow.

thought you might like to know more about Guno and where he lives, and I'm sure your mum will help you find out more from the websites. Well done, Mum!

Best wishes with your enormous project,
Maggie (Sarah's mum)

Malawi

Eimer is a nurse in Malawi, and so was in a perfect position to answer Toby's questions about illnesses. Toby had heard of malaria, but never of bilharzia. Both sound really nasty and Toby was glad that Eimer is there in Malawi to help people.

Letter to Eimer

Dear Eimer,
How are you? What illnesses do people get in
Malawi? What food do you eat?
  Bye,
  Toby

Response from Eimer

Dear Toby,
Thank you so much for your letter. It was lovely to
get a letter with interesting questions!
  I am very well, thank you for asking. It is very,
very hot here at the moment and soon it will rain
and rain and rain and all the plants will grow and
the whole country is very green and beautiful then!
  When the rain begins here, the people who live
here start planting crops and farming their land.
One of the big things that they grow here is called
maize. In England we call it corn and mostly it is
yellow and you eat corn-on-the-cob, or sweetcorn.
Maybe you have had these in your tea? Here in
Malawi the maize is white. People make it into

flour and use that flour to make porridge, called phala, which they eat for breakfast, and then they make something called nsima, which is white and very solid and you eat it with your hands! You take a piece of nsima and make it into a ball, squashing it with your hand and then dip it into sauce and eat it. Malawians eat nsima *every* day, sometimes twice a day for lunch and for dinner. It is very, very filling and keeps you full all day.

Malawians also really enjoy eating potatoes – but only when they are chips! They like them very, very salty – so salty that it would burn your tongue and make you want to drink lots and lots of water!

You asked me what illnesses people get in Malawi. They get lots of the same illnesses that you get in the UK, like upset tummies and head-aches, but here there are a few things that people get that can make them very sick. One of the big illnesses that people can get here is called malaria. It comes from mosquitoes, which bite people at night.

If you're lucky, they just make you itchy, but sometimes you can get malaria from them and it can make you quite poorly. People with malaria get very, very hot – they have a fever and they ache all over, like they have the flu. Sometimes people have to go to hospital to get medicine in their veins because they are too poorly to take tablets. Mosquitoes like water, so there are more people sick with malaria in the rainy season when there is water everywhere, and then the hospital gets very busy. So busy that sometimes patients have to sleep on the floor because there are not enough beds for everybody!

There is one other disease that is very common here – it's called bilharzia (bit difficult to say!). This disease comes from snails that live in the lake here. It is crazy common because the lake is *so, so* big! And because everybody swims in the lake, has showers in the lake, washes their clothes in the lake and some people have to drink the water straight from the lake as well. This disease makes your tummy hurt and makes your wee go a funny colour!

There is medicine that you can take to make it better but lots of people here don't have very much money, or live too far away from the doctor so they find it difficult to get better.

I hope that I have answered your questions and

that you enjoyed getting a letter from Malawi!
Good luck with the rest of your project!

    Bye-bye,

    Eimer ☺

PS Here is a present for you from Malawi – it's a bracelet in the colours of the Malawian flag, red, black and green.

Swaziland

After Cathy sent her letter, we spent a long time chatting
about whether it would be good or bad to be asked to
marry the king. Cathy's letter showed us that in many
countries there are things that are very similar to Toby's
life, and other things that are very different too.

Letter to Cathy

Dear Cathy,
How are you? Is only the king allowed to have more than one wife? Do you know any girl who has done the Reed Dance? What food do you eat?
    Bye,
    Toby

Response from Cathy

Hi Toby,
Thank you for your letter. I am very well and hope that you are too. Your handwriting is excellent – you must be doing well at school. Please thank your mum for me for the postcard. I was very interested to hear about your project and hope it is going well. How many countries have you received letters from now?
    We live on a small farm and have 6 dogs, 3 cats, 6 horses, 9 koi, lots of goldfish and a bird. The bird is a black-capped lorikeet called Captain Jack Sparrow (have you seen the film *Pirates of the*

Caribbean?). He can say 'Cap'n Jack', 'Hello' and 'Stop it'.

We have some chalets on the farm, which we let to guests coming from all over the world so they can stay in Swaziland for a few days and enjoy this lovely country. It is my job to organize the bookings and look after the guests while they are here.

Traditionally in Swazi culture a man can have as many wives as he wants, and many, many children. A lot of the older men do have several wives, but the younger men are realizing that it is very expensive to have lots of children, to pay for their food, clothes and education, so more and more of them are deciding to have just one wife. King Mswati now has about 15 wives and a large number of children. I am not sure of the number exactly, but the oldest ones are older than some of his wives! I think he chose a new wife at the Reed Dance this year.

I do not know any girls who have danced in the Reed Dance recently. Some of my friends did so when they were young girls and say it was a very colourful and exciting event. A lot of families do not want their daughters to do the Reed Dance because they want them to concentrate on their education and a career. If the king chooses a girl to be his wife she has to give up everything that she planned to do to marry the king.

My family eats food very similar to yours I expect. We have big supermarkets here just like Sainsbury's or Tesco. They stock most of the foods you get in England. The Swazi people mainly eat a kind of very stiff porridge made from maize meal (maize is a variety of sweetcorn). They have it with a sauce made from vegetables like onions, tomatoes and spinach, and sometimes some meat grilled over an open fire. They also eat bread, rice, beans, eggs, fruits like pawpaws and bananas, and they like to drink tea with lots of sugar and milk, but most of them do not drink coffee. When we have a party here at the farm for the people who work for us at Christmas, they like to eat LOTS of braaied (here we call it a braai not a barbeque) meat and chicken with salads and coleslaw and have LOTS of Coca-Cola and lemonade for a treat.

I am enclosing with this letter a copy of the magazine *Swaziland Discovery*. It is a magazine produced for the tourists who visit Swaziland and has some information about the country and lots of nice photos. I hope you enjoy looking through it.

Wishing you good luck with your project. I look forward to hearing how you get on.

With best wishes,

Cathy

Buhleni Farm, Swaziland

Tanzania

Jean's letter was a very early one, and Toby has wanted
to learn to dive ever since! He was amazed by her
drawing skills, and it was also the first time he heard
of a nature conservationist. Jean also very casually
says, 'If you ever come to Tanzania', which was probably
the first time Toby considered that all these places he
was writing to might be places he could visit one day.
It made them much more real, and immediately
spiralled out of control as he decided that pretty
much every country in the world would need visiting!

Letter to Jean

Hi Jean,
How are you? Can you dive? What is the most amazing sea creature you have ever seen? What is your job?
Bye,
Toby

Response from Jean

Dear Toby,
Thank you so much for your letter! I am so excited and happy to be a part of this wonderful thing you are doing. I hope you learn lots from the different countries!

So let's get straight to answering the questions, shall we? Do I dive? I do not scuba-dive, which is where you use a tank full of oxygen to be able to go deep under the water for a long time. I do, however, love snorkelling, and go out often to swim over the reefs near Kilwa. The colours are so beautiful! I can spend hours floating above the coral and looking for new species of fish, starfish, crayfish and coral that I have not yet seen.

The strangest creature that I have ever seen was a purple jellyfish – I sent a photo of it to try and describe it better. It looked like a purple see-through soccer ball with lumps all over it, which was wearing a rusty brown skirt! It looked like it could have been made out of rubber or plastic. I did not see it while diving but in the shallow water while walking along the beach. Nature really does have some magnificent creatures!

A couple of interesting or not so interesting facts about me – my favourite colour is green, I LOVE mangoes, I have never lived in a city before, the first place I ever went to abroad was England, I love nature and hope to work as a nature conservationist one day.

The job that I do at the moment is managing a small lodge on the coast overlooking the mangroves. I also volunteer with some small conservation NGOs.

If you ever come to Tanzania, you should definitely see the Serengeti National Park and Ngorongoro Crater. Go and see Ol Doinyo Lengai (a semi-active volcano holy for the Masaai tribe), eat the delicious fruit on the coast and sail on a dhow (a local sailing boat used on the east African coastline).

I hope you eventually receive this and it doesn't get lost in the African postal system! Good luck with all the letter writing!

I will be following you online!

With lots of salaams and best wishes,

Jean

Togo

Stephanie teaches at an international school, and her class was just a little bit older than Toby when they responded. We loved that they all told us something about themselves and their lives. It prompted us to think about how tricky it is to say just one thing about yourself!

Letter to Stephanie

Dear Stephanie,
How are you? Have you been to Tamberma Valley?
What food do you eat? What is your school like?
What do the children do for the service in the
community programme?
   Bye,
   Toby

Response from Stephanie

Dear Toby and family,
I hope both the postcards make their way to you!
My class were very excited to receive your letter and
wanted to tell you more about Togo/our class:

- Aensa – Our school uniform is blue.
- Ted – We sometimes have chips and a burger for
  lunch.
- Sarah – It is always hot.
- Emrys – I love rice. It's yummy.
- Jason – There are 14 people in our class.
- Yannis – I like football.

- Ella – I live on the beach.
- Nathan – I cycle to school.
- Keerthanaa Shri – I have the longest name in the class.
- Geraud – People call me J.J.
- Esoliim – I know my 5 x table.
- Ephraim – I have 2 dogs.
- Rohey – I speak French.
- Hamza – I love chocolate.

We hope you like our letter,
Stephanie & Year 2

Uganda

This is a letter that went out by 'personal post', thanks to the wonderful Laura. While we were researching the orphanage and the country, Toby realized that many of his questions suggest that people have the funds to travel or pay entrance fees, so in this letter he concentrated more on daily lives, games and food, and the responses helped him understand a bit more about the lives of other children around the world.

Letter to the House of Love orphanage

Dear everybody,
How are you? Do you go to school? Do you have any toys to play with? What food do you eat? What kind of house do you live in?
　Bye,
　Toby

Response from the orphanage

Dear Toby,
We are *kawa* (very fine). What about you? Oh! Thank you for your greetings. Really I liked your photo. Your smart.
　Yes I go to school and I like studing and I am in senior one at a beautiful school called Kichwamba High School and our motto is 'SUCCESS OUR GOAL', but the problem is that I can't afford to have everything like clothes, shoes etc. And I have toys but not enough.
　I had forgot to tell you I wish I should be 'a doctor' and treat people as they are your friends in Uganda.

I like to eat postio, beans, rice, cassava, millet flour, maize, chappate, chocolate biscuits, fish, meat, yams, sorghum, scumawic, banana, ginuts, tomatoes, vegetables. Oh they are very many. If *possible* you can come and we enjoy on them.

Then for houses they are temporary, meaning they are covered with thorny grasses, smeared with clay type of soil. Even they are in bad conditions but nothing to do and even I wish I could come to England but it's not possible.

Goodbye toby but may God keep you with that spirit and I have loved you. If possible keep on with your writings and I shall keep on doing so. Thank you, may God the creator of heaven and earth bless you in your future.

From HOUSE OF LOVE AFRICA
BY NINYESIGA GODFREY
Meaning of name: I trust in 'GOD'.

*

Dear Toby,
How are you and how is your life? For me, I am okay.

Yes! I do go to school. I am in P.5 class.

No I don't have toys to play with and I like banana, sweet potatoes, yams, posho, rice and Irish potatoes.

I live in tempolary house.

My god bless you. Thank you.

I am called Magret.

ASIA

Afghanistan

James is a soldier currently stationed in Afghanistan – he was Toby's third attempt to write to Afghanistan. The first was to a school in Kabul, the second to a US soldier there. We don't know what happened to the first letter, but the second came back as undeliverable. James's letter helped shed a bit of light on the situation in Afghanistan, and in language that made sense to a little boy.

Letter to James

Dear James,

How are you? What do you do in your free time? How do you talk to the local people? Do children play football in the villages? What are you doing in Afghanistan? What food do you eat?

   Bye,
   Toby

Response from James

Hi Toby,

How are you? I am very well, thank you. I have been in Afghanistan for nearly 3 months. I am an army officer and I currently have 24 soldiers that I look after. We are based in Kabul, which is the capital city. Our job is to help the government to look after the people of Afghanistan whilst they build things like new hospitals and schools.

   The previous 2 times I was in a province (a bit like a county) called Helmand. The people there were very poor. They lived in mud houses called compounds. There were some very bad people down there that we had to fight. The locals in Helmand spoke a language called Pashtan, which is spoken in southern Afghanistan and in parts of Pakistan. Here in Kabul most people speak Dari. This is like Farsi, which is spoken in Iran.

The children play football but their favourite sport is cricket. They even made it to the Cricket World Cup this year!

I am lucky that we share our camp with American soldiers so we get lots of nice food. On my other trips here I have eaten with the local people. They mainly have rice and bread with chicken or vegetables.

I am very impressed with your project. It is very inspiring and I am pleased I managed to help you with a country.

James

Bangladesh

Sifat's letter was an early one. Toby would love to go to Bangladesh and see the tigers, but we also loved the way Sifat explained the job of a paediatric surgeon to a (then) five-year-old: 'I fix up sick kids.'

Letter to Sifat

Hi Sifat,
How are you? Have you ever seen a Bengal tiger?
What is food like in Bangladesh?
    Bye,
    Toby

Response from Sifat

Dear Toby,
Hey there, smart boy, how are you? I am fine. Give
your mom and your family my best regards.

    You have already known my name and what
I do. I'll explain some more. My name is Sifat.
I am a doctor. I live in a small town alone, all by
myself. ☹ My family lives in a big city. I work in a
hospital and I am a pediatric surgeon. I fix up sick
kids.

    In our country people are very simple and they
are sometimes not aware of healthy habits so they
become sick. Common sickness here in Bangladesh
is diarrhoea (food poisoning), tuberculosis and a

few tropical diseases. So do you know what are the healthy habits?

In the southern part of Bangladesh there is a forest named Sundarban. It is very beautiful. It is the home of royal Bengal tigers. The royal Bengal tiger is a large, ferocious and very powerful beast. They are beautiful and graceful too. I only have seen them in the zoo. But I always wish to visit the forest and see a tiger in its rightful place, the Sundarban. There is also deer, crocodiles and many birds.

There is a lot of delicious food available here in Bangladesh. Generally we eat rice, lentil soup and different vegetable curries. We eat three times a day. Breakfast is done usually with chapatti (flat bread), egg and vegetable curry and tea of course, and then for dinner and lunch we eat rice. Bangladesh is a riverine country. So plenty of fish is available here. Bangladeshi people love to eat fish. Do you like fish, dear?

Dear Toby, I am very glad to write to you. And I always imagine how do you look. So next time send a picture of you, and I'm sending mine, and some other pictures that will give you some idea about Bangladesh.

We are friends now so write to me soon. I'll be waiting for your letter.

Always be a good boy, listen to your parents and be kind and gentle to your friends.

With love,

Sifat

Fardipur

Bhutan

Ugyen's and Jamtsho's mum told us both boys were very keen to write to Toby. Since this letter he has written to Ugyen and Jamtsho again, and we have worked out that one letter exchange takes about three months, so hopefully, over time, he will learn lots more about Bhutan.

Letter to Ugyen and Jamtsho

Dear Ugyen and Jamtsho,
How are you? Is Dzongkha a hard language to learn? How do you say 'My name is Toby' in Dzongkha? Do you do lots of art? What is your favourite kind of art? What clothes do you wear? Did you feel the earthquake from Nepal?
    Bye,
    Toby

Response from Ugyen and Jamtsho

Dear Toby,
I am fine. Hope you are fine too. Dzongkha is hard to write but easy to read. I do art sometimes. I like to draw flowers, trees, rivers and mountains. I wear pants and shirts mostly. I felt the earthquake.
What game do you like?
    Bye,
    Ugyen

*

Dear Toby,
I am fine. Hope you are fine too. Dzongkha is hard to write but easy to read. I like doing art like

drawing cartoons. I wear pants and shirts but I like to wear gho most. *Gho* is our national dress. I too felt the earthquake from Nepal.

Bye,
Jamtsho

Brunei

Sometimes, when we research a country, Toby's questions all come out in a big jumble. His letter to Clare is a great example of this. A question about religion is followed directly by 'Have you ever eaten anything wrapped in a leaf?' And, of course, Toby wants to visit 'the building with a teapot on top'!

Letter to Clare

Dear Clare,
How are you? Do you cover your hair? Do lots of Muslim people live in Brunei? Have you ever eaten anything wrapped in a leaf? Can you eat the leaf? Have you seen the sultan? What is the building with a teapot on top?
    Bye,
    Toby

Response from Clare

Dear Toby,
I hope you are well? What an amazing project you have started! I hope this letter from Brunei ticks another country off the list for you. I have lived here for 8 years now, but used to live in Surrey!
    It is very exciting in Brunei at the moment as we are waiting for the Hari Raya holidays to start, when the moon is sighted. It has the same atmosphere as Christmas – there are festive lights up all over town and lots of sales in the shops!
    There are only 450,000 people in Brunei and the

majority are Muslim, but there are lots of Chinese Bruneians and expats that live here too – and we all get invited to join the celebrations. The sultan opens his palace for 2 days too and you can meet him if you are a boy; girls queue separately and meet his wife. I have been – it was amazing, but I had to queue for 3 hours!

Only Muslims cover their hair here, so I do not have to. At school the girls have the choice – many want to, but some do not. However, that is an international school, in local schools girls wear a headscarf, but always have their faces on show!

I have seen the sultan a few times as he drives around and if you wave, he is very friendly and waves back! We are very lucky as he is a very kind and generous man. We all hope this continues when he hands over to his son. We do not know when this will happen!

I often eat chicken that has been wrapped in banana leaf to be cooked. You don't eat the leaf but it keeps the chicken really moist and tasty! My favourite foods are beef rendang and nasi lemak!

We are very lucky because Brunei is beautiful and we often take trips to the rainforest – where we see lots of animals, including monkeys, crocodiles and snakes. Sometimes you get monkeys in the garden – but we don't like that, even though it sounds exciting. When there is a poisonous snake near your home you are allowed to call the fire brigade – 'the Bomba' – and they will take the snake away back to the jungle.

I think the building 'with the teapot' is the mosque that was built for the last sultan. They are so beautiful and full of gold and expensive fittings.

I hope you have exciting things planned for your school holidays. We are very lucky as we get to travel lots in our holidays and Asia is so lovely to travel in!

I hope I have answered all your questions, and I hope you get your project completed soon.

From,

Clare x

Brunei Darussalam

China

Toby's first letter to China (which is included in the photo section) actually went to Hong Kong and his contact there, Tiwei, wrote her response in both English and Mandarin. He became fascinated by the language and culture. In summer 2014 Sheffield had a Chinese summer school, where children could spend a week learning a bit of Mandarin, but also try dancing, food, watch films and make art. It was run by the Confucius Institute, who help people all over the world learn Chinese. Toby loved it, and asked to keep up with lessons. He has been learning Mandarin ever since, and is loving it. To make sure mainland China is also represented, we are also sharing some letters from the International School of Wuxi. China is one country Toby is definitely planning to visit when he is older.

Letter to the International School of Wuxi

Dear everybody,

How are you? What is your school like? Have you been to the Grand Buddha at Ling Shan? What do you do after school? What food do you eat?

    Bye,

    Toby

Response from Miss McKee and the kindergarten class

Dear Toby,

Thank you for letting us participate in this project!

    We are the only kindergarten class in our school (small school). There are 15 kids in our class from 5 different countries – China, America, Japan, Korea & Hong Kong.

    Our school is from 9:15 – 3:30 every day, and everyone eats the school's lunch.

    We have classes for kids from 3 years old to 12th grade.

    I have not been to the Grand Buddha at Ling Shan, but I think some of our high-school students went there on a field trip a few years ago for one of their classes. We have many types of food served in our cafeteria from our 3 biggest represented countries – Korea, China & America. We eat lots of rice (every day), soup (every day) and other things like pizza, stir-fry, bulgogi (Korean dish of beef, onions, carrots and sauce), meats, breads and so much more.

I have included some pictures for you as well. The really big one is from November on International Day. We dress up in an outfit from our home country. The one with 4 ladies in dresses is also from International Day. Since America doesn't have a traditional outfit, we wore historical dresses. I'm on the left in a Colonial America dress, the next lady is wearing a Pilgrim's outfit, the next is a Pioneer outfit, and then another Pilgrim outfit.

Under that is 5 of our teachers at a place called Moon Hill in Yangshuo, China. VERY gorgeous place! The last page is from a cave we (the 5 teachers) visited. They have colorful lights shining on some of the rock formations. The one on the bottom is supposed to look like a peacock . . .

Once again, thank you for letting us participate

in your Writing to the World project!! You are a
very ambitious young man!

Zài jiàn! (Goodbye!)

Nín de péng yǒu (your friends), Miss McKee's
kindergarten class (Jaden, Viviana, Shekinah,
Kensuke, Kai, Dana, Hiroshi, Ava, Ethan, Ji Won,
Lucy, Scarlett, Amy, Sarah & Ilir)

*

Dear Toby,

My name is Viviana. I am from Korea. My skol is
called ISW. It is green and wit. After skol I have
Korean Club. What is England lik? <3

Your friend,

Viviana

India

Toby has written quite a few letters to India – eventually he is hoping to cover all states and territories, like he did with the USA, Canada and Australia. It is very hard to choose a letter, so we are sharing the first. Ramesh and his daughter gave Toby a lovely introduction to such a diverse country, and Tanya sent us lots and lots more information – we don't think Toby will ever get bored with India!

Letter to Ramesh

Hi Ramesh,
How are you? Did you get coloured powder thrown at you at the Holi festival? Have you been inside the Charminar?
    Bye,
    Toby

Response from Ramesh

Hello Toby,
Wish you a very happy new year.
    Thank you for writing to me.
    India is a very big united country that is culturally divided into many regions. North India, North-east India, East India, South-west India, West India and Central India. Each of the above regions in India have their own language, food and weather.
    Some festivals are celebrated across the entire country. And some festivals are celebrated only in a few parts of the country. The festival of colours (called Holi) is usually celebrated in the north and

west of India. The festival of lights (called Diwali) is celebrated in most parts of India, but not in some parts of south India. The festival of harvest is celebrated across all parts of India under different names.

Christmas is celebrated across all India. I hope you had a good Christmas. What did Santa Claus gift you?

I am sending you a book on India and I hope you will like it. I am also sending you a map of India where I have pointed out the city I live.

I had been inside Charminar a few years ago.

Ramesh

*

Letter to Tanya

Dear Tanya,
How are you? Have you been to the Lotus Temple? Do you wear a sari? Have you been to the Taj Mahal?

Bye,
Toby

Response from Tanya

Dear Toby,

Here are some facts not many people know about the Taj Mahal:

1. It took 21 years and over 22,000 people to make it!
2. The Taj Mahal appears to be a different colour at different times of the day!
3. It looks exactly the same from each of its 4 sides!

I really hope that you will visit India and see it yourself one day.

The Lotus Temple looks so pretty! I must say, inside, it is very very quiet. Unlike Delhi roads, which are very noisy! You can see cars, autorickshaws and even cows on the roads.

The Jantar Mantar is actually an observatory! It is one of 5 of its kind. The other 4 are at Jaipur, Ujjain, Varamasi and Mathusa. It was built in the 1720s by Maharaja (that means great king) Jai Singh II who loved mathematics, architecture and astronomy. Each of the buildings in the photo is actually a giant instrument (they didn't have telescopes that time, sadly). Jantar means instrument and mantar means formula.

Chaat is a (very yummy) type of snack food. This is my mum's recipe for 'Chana Chaat'.

1. To boiled chickpeas, add 1 chopped onion, 1 tomato and cilantro (coriander).
2. Add salt, red chilli powder and cumin powder as per taste.
3. Squeeze some lemon juice and you're done! In case you want to alter the taste, feel free.

I hope you like it!

Fruit chaat:
To chopped fruit (e.g. banana, apple, guavas, pears, orange, grapes etc), add chaat masala (easily available at a supermarket or asian grocery store). Add salt and sugar to taste.

Indonesia

---

*Toby's letter to Karenina coincided with Ramadan 2015.
In fact, Karenina wrote her letter on the third
day of Ramadan, and it arrived with us just a couple
of days before Eid. It was the perfect time for us to
learn a bit more about it, and we ended up going to a
local Eid festival. We also cooked Karenina's
recipe, nasi goreng, and it was delicious!*

Letter to Karenina

Dear Karenina,

How are you? Can you go up the Monas? What food do you eat in Indonesia? Please can you send us a recipe? Have you been to the kite museum? How do you say 'My name is Toby' in Indonesian? What is school like in Indonesia?

Bye,

Toby

Response from Karenina

Dear Toby

I'm fine, splendid actually.

Today is my 3rd day fasting. Fasting is a duty for Muslims around the world during a period called Ramadhan. We cannot eat or drink and do good from morning till dawn. Hope you are having a fine day btw.

Yes we can! But the last time I went up to Monas is when I was your age. Now I am 16. We have various kinds of food here. My favourite is black pepper crab meat! But common foods that are eaten by people here is nasi goreng, or in English it's called fried rice.

Nasi Goreng Spesial

2 tablespoons sweet soy sauce
2 tablespoons tomato sauce
1 teaspoon salt
½ teaspoon sugar
½ teaspoon shrimp paste (in Indonesian: *terasi*)
2 chilis
4 plates of rice (cooked)
100g chicken breast, diced, fried
200g of shrimp (cleaned)

Heat the butter, insert all of the spices and the chilis (mashed), stir until it smells. Put in the rice, chicken & shrimp. Mix them until they're even.

Do send me the recipe of your favourite dish in the UK! Yes! I've been to the kite museum here. There are lots of wonderful & colourful kites here. When I was your age I can't fly a kite. I suck at it! :P

'My name is Toby' = *Nama saya Toby.*

School here is great! We have our own uniforms depending on our level in school. What I love most about school is the cafeteria! It's very different here, the cafeteria. We have to buy our own food. So there are many sellers there. Buying food in school is called *Jajan.*

We have many sellers too outside the front gate of school. People sell lots of cool things like baby chickens, snails (for pet), water balloons and foods too! What do you like most about your school and what's your favourite subject? Personally, I HATE math, and I am always terrible at it :P. My sister is taking her masters degree in Southampton BTW! I never visit UK before but I heard UK is very nice & peaceful. Indonesia is a very hot & crowded country, but the people here are very friendly! ☺

Love,
Karenina
Bye

Iraq

We weren't sure where exactly to place this letter in the book, but it did go to Iraq, so that's where we are sharing it. Toby wrote to a Syrian boy, Dilan, living in a refugee camp in Iraq. ShelterBox, one of the charities Toby is supporting with his project, contacted us and told us that one of their volunteers would be able to take a letter to Dilan, and also bring the response back. It was an amazing opportunity, and we are very grateful to ShelterBox for helping us!

Letter to Dilan

Dear Dilan,
How are you? I am sorry you had to leave your home.
Are you OK? Is it hard playing the tambur? What do
you write your songs about? What do you want to be
when you grow up? What food do you eat?
  Bye,
  Toby

Response from Dilan

Hi Toby,
Thank you very much. My warm greetings for you.
I'm very happy to receive your letter, which supported
me a lot. I hope that I'm going to be an international
artist. I wish you a nice future and that we are going to
be friends for you. Keep in touch.
  Thanx

Japan

*Sabine knew Joseph when he lived in England,
so when Toby started his project, his letter
to Joseph and his wife, Satoko, was among the first
ten to go out. We have stayed in touch with
them, and they now have a little boy themselves.*

Letter to Joseph and Satoko

Hi Joseph and Satoko,

Are you well? What do you like about Japan? I saw the message you wrote in my book – thank you! I have just run 5k. I know you like running too.

Bye,
Toby

Response from Joseph and Satoko

Konnichiwa Toby! (Hello in Japanese)
Thank you so much for your letter. We were very happy to receive it. We are both very well. Today is Sunday so we will be relaxing at home in Tokyo. Later today we will go out to have some sushi (raw fish) at our favourite restaurant – the food in Japan is very tasty! We will take our pet penguin 'Pepe' with us because he LOVES raw fish too!

We love Japan because the people are very friendly, it's clean and the countryside is beautiful with a lot of places to go and explore! This summer I will climb Mount Fuji, the tallest mountain in Japan.

Mount Fuji is actually a volcano, but luckily it seems to be sleeping at the moment. We also like the technology in Japan; robots are becoming popular to help people in their daily lives.

You can [run] 5k?!! Wow! It took me 30 years to train to run 5k, but you have already done it. I'm very impressed! I will go running tomorrow. I enjoyed visiting your house and writing in your book, and I hope we can meet again one day, maybe in Japan!

Please say hello to your mum for us! With love from Tokyo!

Joseph and Satoko

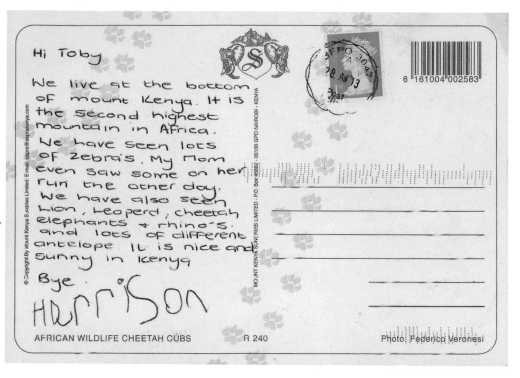

Hi Toby

We live at the bottom
of mount Kenya. It is
the second highest
mountain in Africa.
We have seen lots
of zebra's. My mom
even saw some on her
run the other day.
We have also seen
Lion, Leoperd, cheetah
elephants + rhino's.
and lots of different
antelope It is nice and
sunny in Kenya

Bye.

Harrison

AFRICAN WILDLIFE CHEETAH CUBS   R 240   Photo: Federico Veronesi

Kenya

Toby was amazed to learn that there are children who regularly see
lions, zebras and antelopes, just like he sees magpies and squirrels.

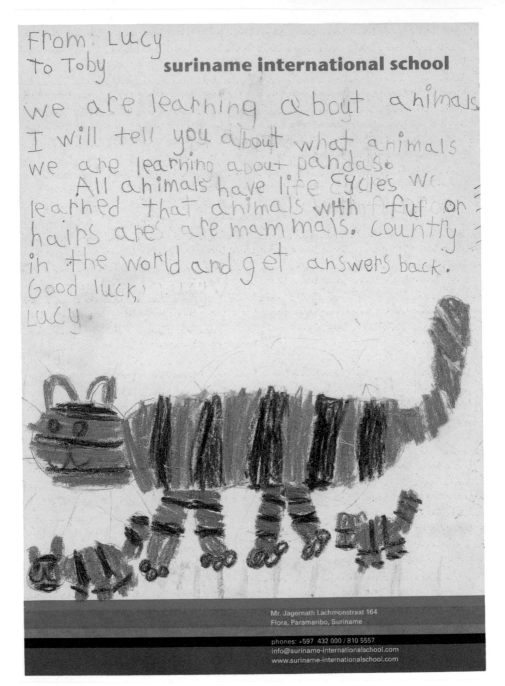

From: Lucy
To Toby   **suriname international school**

we are learning about animals
I will tell you about what animals
we are learning about pandas.
    All animals have life cycles we
learned that animals with a fur or
hairs are are mammals. country
in the world and get answers back.
Good luck, Lucy
LUCY

Suriname

Toby loved reading what they were learning about, which wasn't that different to what he was learning around the same time.

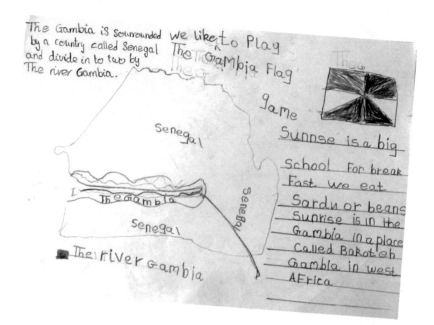

The Gambia is sourounded
by a country called Senegal
and divide in to two by
The river Gambia.

we like to Play
The Gambia Flag

Senegal

The Gambia

Senegal

Senegal

The river Gambia

game
Sunrse is a big
School For break
Fast we eat
Sardu or beans
Sunrise is in the
Gambia in a place
Called Bakoteh
Gambla in west
AFrica

Gambia

The children at the Sunrise
Centre shared their game of
The Flag, which is just like
Tic Tac Toe!

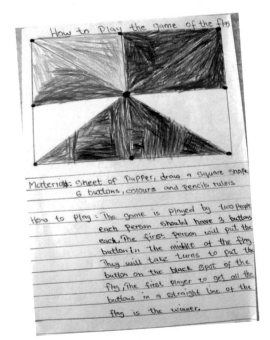

How to Play the game of the flag

Materials: Sheet of Papper, draw a square shape
6 buttons, colours and pencils rulers

How to Play: The game is played by two people
each Person should have 3 buttons
each. The first Person will put the
button in the midire of the flag
They will take turns to put the
button on the black spot of the
flag, The first Player to get all the
buttons in a straight line of the
flag is the winner.

Antarctica

James and his colleagues at the Antarctica research station gave Toby one of the best birthday presents ever – they sent him a special banner along with photos of it being held up at the South Pole!

Philippines

Anika's students created pop-up books to answer his questions, and it is impossible to show all the flaps, levers and pulls in a picture! We are still in touch via Toby's Facebook page and they sent us updates when Typhoon Haiyan hit shortly after this letter exchange.

The students here never get tired of SMILING. ☺ Even through there are lots of HAPPENINGS AND ACTIVITIES to get us busy, we never lose the time to laugh and smile with friends. Hope you enjoy, Toby!

So that's the end of your journey for now, Toby! Hope you had a great time. If you have more questions about our school, please don't hesitate to let us know. Hope you never forget us and know that you will always have a family in us. Thank you and see you someday! ☺
~ ...High Students ^_^

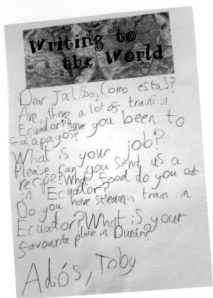

Ecuador

Toby really enjoys learning languages and often uses his letters as a way to try out new sentences.

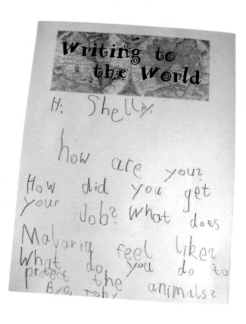

Malawi

The topic of Malaria is often mentioned in letters from Africa, and for a boy in the UK it can be difficult to understand what this might be like.

Benin

We loved this card and the saying on it; it seemed the perfect phrase to sum up Toby's project.

Jordan

Toby loved writing to Anees and Vanessa. We were both fascinated by the city of Petra, and Anees is not only an artist who makes sculptures, he also makes props for films, which Toby decided was a very cool job to have, although Toby's dream would be to be part of an archaeological dig in Petra.

Letter to Anees and Vanessa

Dear Anees and Vanessa,
How are you? Do they do archaeology digs at
Petra? Which bit of Petra do you like best? Does
Petra give you lots of ideas for your sculptures?
How did you get into making props for films?
　Bye,
　Toby

Response from Anees and Vanessa

Dear Toby,
Thank you for your letter. They do many archaeological digs in Petra. In fact, only one third of
Petra has been uncovered; the rest is still to be
dug. The picture on this card is of one of the
biggest monuments, which is my favourite part of
Petra.

　I get many ideas for my sculptures from the
ancient art in Petra and elsewhere, and because I
know how to carve things from stone, wood and
other materials sometimes films ask me to make

their props. I made many stones from foam that looked like real ones and that were dropped on actors in films. We have many amazing places in Jordan; I hope you visit one day.

Anees and Vanessa

South Korea

Toby has written to a lot of schools, but this was the first time he ended up in a school newspaper. After receiving the letters, we looked up some Korean traditional drumming on the internet – it looks very elegant!

Letter to Gyeongseo Middle School

Dear everybody,

How are you? What is your school like? Have you been to Apsan Park and seen the fossilized dinosaur footprints? What food do you eat?

  Bye,
  Toby

Response from Megan

Dear Sabine and Toby,

Thank you so much for the letters you sent to our school. I showed the students a few news stories from the internet about Toby and wrote a short piece about his adventure in our school's English-language newspaper. Unfortunately the newspaper wouldn't fit in this envelope. I have, though, enclosed some stickers for Toby.

  The students were very interested in his story and enjoyed learning how to write a letter in English.

  Our school is on the southern edge of Daegu near the Daegu Arboretum. It was cold here a few weeks ago and even snowed once, but the highs are in the mid-50s this week (around 12 degrees Celsius).

Let me know when you receive this. The students will be delighted. They have been studying hard lately and take their final exams this week. The Korean school year runs from February to December with nearly a month off in January for Chinese New Year. We are all looking forward to the vacation.

Kindest regards,
Megan Kyker

*

Dear Toby,

How are you doing? I'm doing well, but it's getting cold here. Winter will come soon. We have a small school with only 130 students. It's a rural school. We won a drumming contest! I like to go to P.E. class. I like to play badminton. We study from 8 a.m. to 4 p.m.

No I have not been to Apsan Park, but I want to go soon. My favourite food is bibimbap. I eat rice every day. What is your favourite food?

Thank you,
Yebih

Maldives

Toby received this letter when he was five, and the
students' suggestion 'You should really go diving once
you're older', together with other similar letters,
has made him determined to learn to dive as soon
as he can, so he can go and see all the amazing creatures
so many of his writing partners have told him about.

Letter to Sharon

Dear Sharon,

How are you? Have you ever seen a whale shark? What food do you eat? Have you ever been on a seaplane, and if you have, what was it like? I like that all your students are helping in the community.

 Bye,
 Toby

Response from Sharon

Dear Toby,

We are Sharon's students. We are really glad you wrote to us. To answer your questions, we have seen whale sharks, but not in the Maldives. But we see jellyfish, eels, dolphins and even huge manta rays and sharks. Also, we have all been on a seaplane. It is like a flying boat and the view is very pretty because you get to see lots of islands and reefs since seaplanes cannot fly as high as aeroplanes.

 As for what we eat, there are a lot of different

types of food made of fish. Also, Maldivians love to eat spicy food.

You should really go diving once you're older. It's exciting and you get to see lots of colourful fish, as well as corals and other cool things, and we are sure you will have heaps of fun.

We really hope you will visit our country one day. Thank you for the lovely letter.

Take care,

Lamha, Amana, Yasmin, Laisa, Ainnie, Maryam, Raaima and Modith

Mongolia

Sabine has been to Mongolia, so this was another country where we had some family travel stories. She has even been to the British Embassy – but we never knew that there was an embassy cat. Toby particularly loved the very official-looking card.

Letter to Isabelle

Hi Isabelle,

How are you? What does an ambassador do?
What is Mongolia like? Have you been to Turtle
Rock?

   Bye,
   Toby

Response from Isabelle

Dear Toby,

Thank you for your letter. It was lovely to hear
from you.

   We are very well and enjoying the short summer
that Mongolia has, unfortunately only two months
long, with the people in the countryside already
making preparations for the very harsh winter,
which will see temperatures of −50 degrees,
which is very cold indeed.

   Our son, Will, who is 20, is also with us for the
summer, which is lovely. He has been involved in
many projects: meeting Colonel John Blashford-
Snell on his return from an expedition and

spending the day with the British military officers involved with the Multinational Peacekeeping Exercise, Khaan Quest 2013.

Ulaanbaatar, where we live, is the coldest capital city in the world. The population is around 1.3 million people, with around 800,000 people still living in the traditional *gers*. A postcard is on its way to you with a picture of a *ger*, livestock and a Mongolian family.

There is a lot of construction work taking place at the moment, making the city very dusty and noisy, but it is developing so fast that new buildings and roads are badly needed. There is also a new international airport being built 60km outside of the city, which will bring lots more people here.

The ambassador is a very busy person who represents the United Kingdom and Northern Ireland here in Mongolia. He tries very hard to help British companies to do business in Mongolia; he works with the Mongolian government, meeting regularly with the president, prime minister and ministers to get them to support our views on issues about the world.

He tells the Mongolian people about the best of

the UK, culturally, politically and economically, building friendships and understanding.

Every year we celebrate HM the Queen's birthday, inviting Mongolian and British guests to our home. This year we had the Mongolian Military Band play the National Anthem just before they left for Scotland to attend the Edinburgh Tattoo and last year we were fortunate to have members of the Mongolian Paralympic team join us for a piece of Her Majesty's birthday cake, which I had baked earlier.

We also have responsibility for Minnie, the embassy cat, who is 10 years old. She was found as a kitten, injured from a road accident, and the staff adopted her and have looked after her ever since. She spends a lot of time in the ambassador's office, sometimes drinking his tea!

At home, which is called the Residence, we also have our own cat, Morris, who we brought with us from Derbyshire. He is very well travelled, having also lived with us in Japan. He has settled in well and is enjoying chasing the birds and mice he finds in the garden.

We visited Turtle Rock earlier this year and it was really interesting. It is located in Gorkhi-Terelj

National Park, which is a great place for walking and horse riding, although when we visited it was very cold, −35 degrees! The same day we also went to watch a camel polo match, which was great fun.

Thank you again for writing and I hope you enjoyed this brief insight into our life in Mongolia.

With very best wishes,

Isabelle

Wife of HM British Ambassador to Mongolia

Nepal

Ever since the start of the project Toby was fascinated by Nepal and Mount Everest. During Toby's project Nepal was hit by a number of disasters, and one of the ShelterBoxes Toby raised money for went there to help a family in need.

Letter to Prabin

Dear Prabin,
How are you? Have you climbed in the Himalayas?
What food do you eat in Nepal? What is your job?
What is the best thing about living in Kathmandu?
  Bye,
  Toby

Response from Prabin

Dear Toby,
Warm greetings from Himalayan country!
  I am glad to receive your mail. Here, we are all
fine, living in Kathmandu, capital of Nepal, with
my family and with my son like you named Arnav
(4 yrs old).
  Himalaya is bit far away from the place I live and I
have been to the mountain region up to 4,000m above
the sea level around Annapurna area (one of the most
popular trekking areas in Nepal after Everest).
  In Nepal we normally eat steamed/boiled rice,
lentil soup, seasonal vegetables and meat (chicken/
pork/buffalo/fish/goat/duck/lamb). During festival

we prepare different variety of food. Among children, momo/chomin are popular. Momo is a dumpling dish made of flour and meat. Also one can prepare with sweet, and vegetable with mushroom.

I work in a travel agency and my duty is to organize/operate different tour packages within Nepal/India/Bhutan & Tibet as well.

Kathmandu (city of glory) being a cultural city, one can enjoy lots of festivals and the climate is very nice and pleasant, not so cold during winter and even not hot during summer.

Write me if you would like to know more about Nepal.

Have a nice day!

With lots of love from Nepal.

Prabin

Russia

We know that Moscow itself is in Europe, but since most of Russia is in Asia, that is where it features on Toby's website — we don't mean to offend anybody! Toby loves St Basil's Cathedral; we have even built a model of it — but thanks to Julia's letter we now know why most photos show it from the outside!

Letter to Julia

Hi Julia,
How are you? Have you ever been inside St Basil's
Cathedral? How do you keep warm in winter?
    Bye,
    Toby

Response from Julia

Dear Toby!
How are you?
    Want you to know that St Basil is not as beauti-
ful inside. Just stone. But imagine that every stone
there has its history!
    And if you ever come to Russia in winter, be sure
to have your warm clothes with you! Wool polover
(is that a correct spelling?!), mittens for sure and a
warm hat! When you have warm clothes on you
can play with snow outside.
    Say hi to your mum from me.
    Your Russian friend,
    Julia

Sri Lanka

Sam not only drew our attention to a problem many
countries have with wild or abandoned dogs, she
also took pictures of her response going to the
post office in Sri Lanka, which was a tiny bit
like going there for a visit, Toby says.

Letter to Sam

Hi Sam,
How are you? Why are there so many street dogs
in Sri Lanka? Can you still tell there was a tsunami
in 2004?
    Bye,
    Toby

Response from Sam

Hi Toby,
Thank you so much for your letter. I was so excited
when the postman arrived with it.
    You have asked some really great questions ☺
    There are lots of dogs living here in Sri Lanka.
Some of them don't have owners at all and they are
on the streets all the time. Some of the dogs do
have owners but not all of the houses have fences so
the dogs can walk where they like.
    I work for Dogstar Foundation and one of my
jobs is teaching people about animals and how to
care for them. We have a colouring book for chil-

dren so I have sent you a copy. I hope you like colouring in as much as I do.

People in Sri Lanka speak three languages, Sinhala, Tamil & English. The colouring book has writing in Sinhala & English. Sinhala uses a different alphabet and it looks really hard to read & write.

The tsunami was a really, really big wave caused by an earthquake in the ocean. The wave damaged a lot of buildings & hotels at the beaches. Most of the damage has been fixed now.

Thanks again for your letter. I really enjoyed reading it & answering your questions.

Sam ☺

Thailand

We first 'met' Kung via Toby's Facebook page, where she responded to many of Toby's posts with examples from Thailand. She told us about Loy Krathong, a Thai festival where you make a flower-decorated basket and float it down the river, so it can take worries and bad luck away from you. Toby loves anything crafty, so we made our own krathong here in England. She also shared recipes and other craft ideas with us — we spent many hours crafting and cooking happily because of Kung!

Letter to Kung

Dear Kung,
How are you? Thank you for all your help with my project. Did you have a good time at the Loy Kra-thong? Do you have to look out for poisonous animals where you live? What is your job?
   Bye,
   Toby

Response from Kung

Dear Toby,
Thank you very much for your letter. During this special period in Thailand, it may take quite long time for any letter sending abroad. So I was quite hesitant to send you this reply letter.
   I am a technical translator who translates a large pile of technical documents from English to Thai. It sounds like a boring job? Yes, but if you like you would learn the newest technology every day. However the bad part is everybody would think that I must be an English language expert, which is not true.

My background is chemical engineering, so if you want to know where is the petrol come from, I may be able to give you some ideas.

In Thailand we celebrate many festival throughout the whole year. Thai people love enjoyment, entertainment and amusement. For example, we have New Year Party of Jan. 1st, Chinese New Year around end of Jan. to beginning of Feb. and Thai New Year on Apr. 13th. You see we celebrate New Year 3 times!

On Loy Krathong day I went to Loy Krathong at Bang Phra Reservoir close to my home. A lot of people come to *loy krathong* and some to *loy komloy*. *Komloy* is a kind of lantern flying in the sky like a hot-air balloon.

Last Jan. 31st was Chinese New Year. I am Thai-Chinese so my family celebrated the season. The season take 3 days long. During the period it is prohibited to say any bad words and do or even think of any bad things.

The 1st day of the season is a day before year end. It is 'Shopping Day'. All Chinese would shop, shop and shop. (Ha ha ha.) What they buy are stuff for sacrifice.

The 2nd day is the 'Sacrifice Day', to gods, to

forlorn spirits (ghosts who did not have any relatives) and to ancestors. The sacrifice stuff are food made of pork, duck, chicken, fish, squid, fruits and silver-gold papers. Each type of meats, fruits and stuffs have their own meaning. It take all day to cook and to sacrifice. At the end they would burn the silver-gold papers and fire the firecrackers.

The last day is the most fun. It is 'Enjoyment Day' or the 1st day of New Year. All parent would take their children to visit grandparent and older relatives to say *'Sin Jia You Ei, Sin Nee Huad Chai'* (Happy New Year, Flourishing New Year) or other good Chinese words. The grandparents and all adults would give money in red envelope, [and] call *'Ang Pao'* (red envelope) to the children. The more relatives you visit the more *Ang Pao* you received! (Ha ha ha) (I also include *Ang Pao* for you with this letter. ^_^) The adult also give *Ang Pao* to their parents as well.

Now, come to your question on poisonous animals.

Yes, there are some poisonous animals here around my home. The most scary ones are cobra. There are snakes visit my home sometime. Most of them are non-poisonous green snakes. But some of

250

them are large cobra, very scary. Thanks to my dog for chase them away.

One of the unusual snake that visit my home was a very large python. During the midnight to dawn, the python was climb on tree, on fence, into my fish pond and finally go out. My dog were very angry but I keep them in house to make sure they would not be eaten by the python.

Other poisonous are giant scorpion and centipede. There are more centipede than giant scorpion hiding under stone in garden. So I have to be careful whenever I work on my garden.

Bye,
Kung

Turkmenistan

We often hear from schools that have used Toby's letters as a lesson aid – either to teach letter writing or to learn a bit about the UK, but this letter helped the children learn something about their own country. When Toby asked about local monuments, the teacher took this as an idea for a class trip, visiting some with the children so that they could draw them and learn about them, and then share their work with Toby!

Letter to Ashgabat International School

Dear everybody,
How are you? Have you been to the Gate to Hell at Derweze? Can you tell me about the Earthquake Memorial in Ashgabat? What is your school like?
  Bye,
  Toby

Response from Ashgabat International School

Dear Toby,
Thank you for your letter. We are good. We loved your letter.
  Some of us have been to Darvaza (the fire crater). It is very cool. A few of us went camping to the fire crater. It was a lot of fun making paper airplanes and flying them into the middle of the crater. We thought they would explode and catch on fire, but they did not. The airplanes ended up flying very high above the crater. Did you know it has been burning for 40 years?
  Yesterday (Monday Oct. 7th) was Memorial Day,

commemorating the 65th anniversary of the earth-quake. Because it was Memorial Day and because you asked about the memorials we went on a class trip to see two memorials in Ashgabat. We drew you pictures of what we saw. We hope you like them.

Because of your letter our 5-year-old-class made it into our school's newsletter. We have sent a copy of the newsletter.

We hope you like the pictures we drew of the monuments. The monument with the bull was so big.

We like our school in Ashgabat. It is a small school and we like it when the Big Kids (high-school kids) come to our class and do fun things with us. What is your school like?

Your friends,

Ashgabat International School 5-Year-Old-Class

OCEANIA

Australia

Emma lives in Melbourne, and in our research, we found out that there is still gold to be found in Warrandyte State Park. Toby was ready to pack his bags and seek his fortune.

Letter to Emma

Dear Emma,
How are you? Have you ever found gold at Warrandyte State park? What is your favourite place in Victoria? What is it like living in Melbourne?
　Bye,
　Toby

Response from Emma

Hi Toby,
Thanks for the letter! I'm good, how are you?
　I have never found gold at Warrandyte. I might have to look next time I go there.

My favourite place in Victoria is Mt. Dandenong. From the top of the mountain there is a great view looking over the city. Driving there in the autumn is so pretty because the leaves on the trees are changing colour.

Melbourne is good because you don't have to go far to see lots of interesting things. The city is close or you can drive an hour and get into rural Victoria where there are lots of paddocks. Even the snow is close in winter, about 2 hour's drive!

In Melbourne there are lots of art galleries and museums to look at. I'm still yet to see them all!

Well done at writing to all the places in the world and I enjoy following you on Facebook to see your news.

From Emma ☺

Marshall Islands

Many of the Pacific Island nations we researched
brought us face to face with climate change.
The idea that whole countries will have to move if sea
levels continue to rise seems far removed from a little
boy living on top of a hill in the UK, but the
letters Toby received made this problem very real.

Letter to Irene

Dear Irene,
How are you? Do you get many storms? Can you dive? Do people travel between the islands a lot? What do you teach at the university? Has anybody ever walked all the way round the atoll?
Bye,
Toby

Response from Irene

Hello Toby,
Thank you for your letter. We are two archipelagos of coral atolls and islands – *Ralik* (sunrise) and *Ratak* (sunset). They have different chiefs but language and customs are the same. We are a large ocean state but the land is limited and precious.

You asked about the weather – we do have storms (last night there was a big one!) but it is never cold here as it is close to the equator. Climate change is a big worry for us and there will be a big conference here about that next year. If the sea level rises one meter, then the islands will flood, food crops will die and eventually the land will disappear. That will mean that the people will have to move.

I hope you read about the Marshalls on the internet. We teach all subjects using distance learning.

Best,

Irene

Nauru

Nauru is the third-smallest microstate in the world (after Vatican City and Monaco). Fewer people live there than in our nearest town. Toby was fascinated by the idea of walking all the way round a country – Adam told us it would take about 3–4 hours, and we have been on longer walks than that!

Letter to Adam

Dear Adam,
How are you? Have you ever walked all the way round Nauru? What are traditional Nauru clothes made from? What food do you eat? Can everybody swim?
    Bye,
    Toby

Response from Adam

Hello Toby,
Thanks for your letter and postcard. I don't think we have got much mail from the UK before ☺
    My family and I are well, thanks for asking. We have been Baptist missionaries on Nauru for 5 years now and really enjoy living on our little island out in the middle of nowhere. I have a wife, Christie, and 3 boys, Elijah, 7, Titus, 3, and Gideon, 15 months.
    Now to your questions . . .
    No, I never have walked round the whole island. I should sometime but haven't yet. My wife has

ridden her bike round it a few times in under an hour. It takes 3–4 hours to walk and is about an 18km trip, best done early in the morning or late in the afternoon as it is very hot during the heat of the day.

Traditional clothes are made of coconut palm branches and other vegetation worn with wreaths or lays made from frangipani flowers. They are only worn for special occasions. Most people wear normal clothes all the time.

All of our food is imported. Most Nauruans eat rice for at least one meal a day. Local food is coconut fish (raw tuna in coconut milk and lime juice), noddy birds (small terns that live on Nauru and eat small fish with the tuna schools . . . they taste like fishy chicken. I don't really like them, but most locals do), and fish.

There are lots of fishermen on Nauru, me and my boys included. Here is my 7-year-old Elijah with his biggest wahoo of 11kg; Titus is next to him. Catching noddy birds is fun. You go up topside (the middle of the island) before dark and set up a stereo that plays sounds of noddy chatter and squawking and they come in at dark and hover to check out the sounds and you scoop them out of the air with a big net on a stick. I think catching them is more fun than eating them; I think that about fish too ☺

Fruit and veggies come in by ship every 6 weeks and plane weekly. There are some fruits grown on the island like mango (we have a big tree in our yard), bananas (we have a few of those too) and breadfruit (they get about the size of a soccer ball). We sometimes make chips with the breadfruit and have fish and chips . . . it's really good ☺

Not everyone can swim, but most can. The kids love going down to the beach in the evening and swimming till sunset. They just recently started a surf club and the kids are getting into surfing.

Here is Elijah's first sailfish, it was 20.5kg/45lb and took him ½ hour to reel in. We had some for lunch and the rest got eaten too ☺ All fish caught on Nauru get eaten ☺ You will notice that Elijah has his lucky shirt on in both pictures ☺

Well, I hope you enjoy my letter. I am going to send you some postcards from Nauru; one of our church members works at the post office ☺

Thanks again for your letter. I wish you all the best in writing the world.

Adam in Nauru

Palau

Our contact in Palau was the education minister, and he kindly agreed to respond to Toby's letter. What we didn't know was that he also forwarded it to teachers and schools in Palau, so we were surprised when we suddenly received a bundle of letters from Palauan school children, featuring lots of drawings of sharks, other sea creatures and the islands. We learned that alii means 'hello' in Palauan, and went through a phase where we greeted each other with a hearty alii! whenever we saw each other, even coming into the room after fetching something from the kitchen. We probably pronounced it wrong . . .

Letter to Palau, via the Ministry of Education

Hi everybody,
How are you? Is it dangerous to swim in the sea?
Have you been on a school trip to the shark sanctu-
ary? What do you do at school?
  Bye,
  Toby

Response from the Director of Education in Palau

Alii, Toby:
It is great getting to know you. Thank you for your
letter. I received it on 16 August. I have not been able
to write back soon as I find myself having so much
work to do. I will be meeting the school principals
for Palau this coming Friday, and so I will be giving
them a copy of your letter and your address so that
they can share them with their students. We will see
if any student will write to you.

Students here have had school field trips to Rock
Islands, a dolphin park, Jellyfish Lake, coral reefs
and other locations, but they have not gone to the
shark sanctuary for safety reasons. I think in time

the students will eventually visit the sanctuary with strict safety measures.

We have alligators and crocodiles in our country too. Students and other people get to see some huge alligators in their pens on land. Perhaps I will get a chance to take a photo of at least one alligator and email it to you.

I have included a picture of some of our students with their brand-new school bus. The students are from Peleliu, an island in Palau famous for a World War II battle between the US and Japan.

Take care, Toby, and I will write again.

Sincerely,

Emery Wenty

Director of Education

Ministry of Education

Republic of Palau

PS *Alii* is the Palauan word for 'hello'.

*

Dear Toby Little,

Hello my name is Dolynn. We love you all. How are you? We know how we know you, because we know you write a letter to our teacher. My teacher read it, so you'll wait for our letters. You'll know we'll wait your letters, because we want to become

271

your friend. We love you all. So take care of yourself. And take care of your home. We love you. We just can be your friend. We love you all, and take good care of the letters, and read my letters carefully, and don't throw it away. It's a good letters, for you.

Thank you

*

Dear Toby Little

Alii! How are you? How is it in England? My name is O'Mara. I'm eight years old. My house in the hillside. But I went to the shark place. My dad drove there. Do you have a father? Do you have a dog? How old are you, Toby? The ocean is not dangerous. It's fun when we swim. Do you live in cold place, that's why you can't swim? We live in a hot place.

God bless you!

Have a nice day all day.

Papua New Guinea

Toby often asks about other languages in his letters, and when we found out that Hiri Motu is spoken in Papua New Guinea he had to learn a little bit. We loved the pictures Juliette sent, because they made us talk about differences in dress-up days when you might pretend to be a princess or a spy, and celebrations where you explore your country's cultural history.

Letter to Juliette

Hi Juliette,
How are you? What is it like being the principal?
How do you say 'My name is Toby' in Hiri Motu?
Do you go diving?
  Bye,
  Toby

Response from Juliette

Dear Toby,
Thank you for writing to me. I have just received
your letter. I was waiting for the letter to arrive
before I would write back to you.

  I am doing very well in Papua New Guinea.

  I am very proud of my school, as we have amazing
children here and also very good teachers. Some are
expat teachers but many are local teachers. I am
learning a lot about Papua New Guinea whilst I am
here. I have only been here over a year, as I have
worked in many different countries over the last 26
years. Being a principal of such a school is a real joy. I
have an amazing job and meet very interesting people.

An international school is always very special as we have many children from different cultures and there is so much to learn from each other. It is very different than education in the UK, but of course we are still teaching the children to read and write just like you. However, we do have very different celebrations.

'My name is Toby' in Hiri Motu goes like this: *Lau ladagu be Toby*. *Lau* means 'my', *ladagu* is 'name', *be* (pronounced with the short vowel sound) is the word 'is'.

I do not dive but I love snorkelling and there are some great places in PNG. I went to the Tufi Resort. You should find that on the internet and see how beautiful it is there.

Hope you are enjoying writing to schools. I think it is a great idea to do that.

Bye,

Juliette

MISCELLANEOUS

While the rest of this book is divided into continents, some letters don't fit quite so neatly into these categories so we've gathered them here. They also happen to include some very special letters and some of Toby's favourites!

Antarctic

We didn't really know who was going to respond when Toby was given an address in France and told that the letter would go to the Antarctic, so this was a special adventure. Even more fun, we could track it heading south from Tasmania on the icebreaker Astrolabe!

Letter to unknown in Antarctica

Hi there,
How are you? What is your name? What is your
job? Where in Antarctica are you? Are you at
Dumont d'Urville? How many people are living
there? Are there fossils there?
   Bye,
   Toby

Response from Mathilde

Hello Toby,
My name is Mathilde. You are a resourceful boy to
write to the Polar French Institute.
   I am a scientist in charge of a LIDAR (Light
Detection and Ranging). It's a laser emitter with a
receptor telescope for studying constituents of the
stratosphere: aerosols and ozone. My work is a part
of a 'study of stratosphere and ozone-layer destruction' program.
   During the winter months, June, July and
August, I tracked the polar stratospheric clouds
who are involved in the ozone-layer destruction

observed during September, October and November when the sun makes a comeback.

I am living at Dumont d'Urville Station. During the wintering we were 25. And now it's the summer season, we are about 50. Winter: March to October and Summer: November to February.

There is no fossils here. But we can find in the ice some shells or algae who were in the seawater before this one freezes to be sea ice.

I wish you well.

Bye,

Mathilde

Antarctic II

We couldn't believe it when James got in touch, and we still can't get over his amazing kindness. James works at the South Pole Research Station, and he went above and beyond to help Toby with his project. Not only did he send a wonderful letter explaining his research and life at the South Pole, he also took pictures of the letter arriving, and of himself holding it. Then, as Toby's sixth birthday was near, he painted a large banner saying HAPPY BIRTHDAY, TOBY and got the whole team to stand and hold it at both South Poles, and sent the pictures to us. He included the banner in his return letter. We don't think we'll be able to ever top this birthday present!

Letter to James

Dear James,

How are you? Why do we need to know about tiny particles in space? Have you seen the Aurora Australis? Are there any children at the South Pole? What do you do for fun? Do you play in the snow? Where do you get your food from? Have you seen a penguin? Are there any palaeontologists working at the South Pole?

    Bye,
    Toby

Response from James

Dear Toby,

I'm excited about your curiosity about the world and the people in it! I imagine you have learned a lot about the world. We need to know about tiny particles a lot, like you want to know about the world. Scientists want to understand about the universe and how it was made. The neutrinos that we study can carry with them information about how they were made. We will learn more about the universe by looking at the sky and seeing tiny particles instead of light.

I'm only at the South Pole during the summer when there are 24 hours of sunlight a day. I have not seen the Aurora Australis, but I have sites I go to see in the northern Arctic. I have seen the Aurora Borealis! It is beautiful!

There are no children at the South Pole. The South Pole could be a dangerous place for kids. There have been children in other parts on Antarctica. One child was even born in Antarctica. Only scientists and the people that keep the station running live here. A few people spend the dark winter here. Nobody can get in or out during the cold, dark winter.

You asked what I do for fun. Yes, sometimes we do play in the snow. Sometimes people make sculptures out of snow blocks. Most of the time we stay inside. We have a gym and a lounge where we can play pool or watch a movie. There is no TV down here. Some people cross-country ski. Last year I played golf outside. I'm sure glad they had an orange ball.

Almost all of our food is flown in on the same airplanes I fly here in. Most of the food is frozen until we need it. They can bring in fresh fruit and vegetables during the summer. We call them 'freshies'. We also have a small greenhouse where we can grow veggies for the winter people.

I have seen penguins! They are cool! Ha! Cool, get it? This year I saw two emperor penguins.

I do not know of any palaeontologists at the South Pole. They study prehistoric life. Nothing but us science people lives at the South Pole. It is too cold and dry to support life, so there is no food for animals. The ice is 3,000 kilometers deep here. Antarctica was once a warm place, though. If there was life, it would be deep under the ice. I'm sure there are palaeontologists in other places in Antarctica where there is not so much ice. They would want to know about early life in Antarctica.

I hope that you stay interested in science! Maybe one day you will be able to come to Antarctica! Stay curious! You've done a wonderful job! I hope you have inspired some other children to do amazing projects and look out at the world around them.

Best of luck in your future!

James

South Pole Station

Summer 2013/14

Connecticut, USA

Like many children, Toby regularly changes his mind about what he wants to be when he grows up, but 'marine archaeologist' combines his love of history and the sea. He has read many books about the Titanic, and was simply over the moon when Dr Ballard agreed to receive a letter from him.

Letter to Dr Ballard

Dear Dr Ballard,
How are you? How old were you when you first thought of finding the *Titanic*? How did you know what you had to learn so that you could get a job where you could find the *Titanic*? Where is *Argo* now? Is it still being used? Was it scary in *Alvin*? Who named all the little submarines and robots? What work do you do now? Have you met Ruth Becker?
   Bye,
   Toby

Response from Dr Ballard

Hello Toby,
I always enjoy getting letters from young children who are so interested in the TITANIC. I always wanted to find the TITANIC but it almost didn't happen. At the same time we were looking for the TITANIC, others were as well; we just happened to be very lucky that the Navy had a secret mission for us to do and then we could look for the

TITANIC when we were done and we are extremely grateful to have been a part of her discovery.

When I was growing up in San Diego, my parents allowed me to explore the shores for hours. I would often look out at the horizon and I wanted to know what was out there and what was deep in the water. When I read the book *20,000 Leagues Under the Sea* by Jules Verne, I knew exactly what I wanted to do when I grew up. I studied math and science and remained focused on my goal. I went on my first expedition when I was 17 years old with Scripps Institution in California and I've been going to sea for over 50 years and it is still exciting to explore.

The ROVs get their names from Greek mythology. ARGUS was the builder of the ship ARGO. JASON was a Greek mythological hero and he was the captain of the ship ARGO. So that's how we came up with the names. That also teaches you a little bit about Greek mythology, which I'm sure you will study in school someday. My ship the NAUTILUS is named after the submarine from the Jules Verne book I mentioned above.

It is always a little bit scary to be in small

submersibles; there is always an element of danger, so that's why we prefer to explore with *Hercules* and *Argus*, which are on my exploration vessel, E/V NAUTILUS. It also takes less time to dive down and return to the surface than if there is a person in the sub. There are still people who go down in the small subs, but I don't think I'll be doing it again.

You asked me what I do for work – I travel all the time and I still go out to sea. I speak at schools and organizations. I love seeing children get interested in the sciences, math and technology.

The NAUTILUS is out to sea now. Who knows what we'll discover in the next couple of months!

I hope that I answered many of your questions, so study hard in school and maybe one day you'll be discovering something special too.

Sincerely,

Dr. Robert D. Ballard

Ecuador

The Galapagos Islands have been Toby's favourite place for a long time, and going there one day is a big dream of his; he is already planning to learn Spanish to make sure he can talk to people there. When school had a dress-up day, Toby dressed up as Charles Darwin. We went to the Natural History Museum in London and he had to see Charles Darwin's notes and exhibits, and take a picture with his statue. Swen Lorenz of the Charles Darwin Foundation very kindly agreed to be a contact for Toby.

Letter to Swen

Dear Swen,
How are you? What is your favourite creature?
Have you met Lonesome George? Do you think
there are any more Pinta Island giant tortoises out
there? Which countries do all your researchers
come from? How could I become a researcher at the
CDF? Can children do research about Galapagos?
Do you have anything from Charles Darwin at the
foundation? What is the last thing about evolution
that you have learned? Why is Galapagos at risk?
    Bye,
    Toby

Response from Swen

Dear Toby,
It was a pleasure to receive your letter, and enclosed
you are finding all the replies to your questions.
    You seem to have a wonderful interest in science
and our planet, and I am sending you my very
best wishes for your birthday and your future
career.

Best regards,
Swen Lorenz
Executive Director, Charles Darwin Foundation

1) What is your favourite creature?

The marine iguana without a doubt! This reptile is a prime example of evolution in action. Its great ancestors arrived here without a food source and had to adapt in order to survive. They go to the sea to find their algae because they have no choice. They either adapt or die. I see them every day here at the research station and they make me smile even when I'm having a bad day.

2) Have you met Lonesome George?

Yes I did, many times, as his living corral was close to the CDF offices. Unfortunately, George is no longer with us, but we think about him a lot and the extinction of the Pinta species is a reminder of why our work is so necessary.

3) Do you think there are any more Pinta Island giant tortoises out there?

We hope so! Probably not on Pinta Island but

we hope that the Pinta DNA is in existence in other giant tortoises on other islands. There are several very interesting projects studying tortoise genetics happening on the islands at the moment and we have our fingers crossed that we might find a George relative someday soon.

4) Which countries do all your researchers come from?

One of the best things about working in the CDF is our mix of nationalities. The majority of our science team are Ecuadorians and we also have scientists from Germany, Spain, Great Britain, the United States, Chile and New Zealand.

5) How could I become a researcher at the CDF?

Finish your school studies, get the highest grades possible, go to university and then find work as a volunteer in conservation to gain experience of working in the field with people from many different places. It is not always an easy process to start a career in conservation but the most important thing to have is passion for what you do and you can't go wrong.

6) Can children do research about Galapagos?

Of course! Children make fantastic scientists and conservationists. Just a few weeks ago the CDF outreach team were in the highlands of Santa Cruz Island working on giant tortoise research with children of many different nationalities. They tracked tortoises with GPS devices as well as inspecting tortoise droppings (don't worry, they don't smell too much!).

7) Do you have anything from Charles Darwin at the foundation?

We do not have any specimens from Darwin's voyage – you need to go to the Natural History Museum in New York or London for that. We have something better – family. Darwin's great-great-grandson Randal Keynes is a CDF board member and friend of our organization. Charles Darwin was fascinated with ancestry and would be delighted that Mr Keynes is a vocal part of the work we do.

8) What is the last thing about evolution that you have learned?

We had a great example here in Galapagos recently and the pictures to prove it! On Fernandina Island, a British scientist saw evidence of land snakes going down to the coast to hunt fish. Again, this is an example of adapting to survive. When I found out about this I couldn't believe it – a land snake fishing for food!

9) Why is Galapagos at risk?

Galapagos is such a fragile ecosystem. Since humans colonized the islands we have introduced species that are harming this wonderful biodiversity. Also, other threats, such as climate change, mean Galapagos animal populations can be easily affected by just the slightest differences in temperature. We have to keep our eye on these problems and continue our work to protect and conserve the archipelago for everyone's benefit.

Greenland

Toby was desperate to write to Greenland, and after several attempts to find a contact, the lovely Paarnaq responded. We made her recipe of kalaallit kaagiat, and it tasted delicious!

Letter to Paarnaq

Dear Paarnaq,
How are you? What is the building in the flag of Nuuk? How do you say 'My name is Toby' in Kalaalisat? Please can you send us a Greenlandic recipe? Do you like it when it is light at night? Do you get the Northern Lights? Would you like to have trees in Greenland?
    Bye,
    Toby

Response from Paarnaq

Dear Toby,
I am doing fine. It's very nice now that the winter is finally over, although we still have a little snow in the mountains.
    Actually it's not the flag of Nuuk, it's the city arms: the building is Ilinniarfissuaq, Greenland's eldest university, built in 1897. Teachers get their education there.
    We actually pronounce 'Toby' just like how you would pronounce it. ☺

I'm sending you a recipe called kalaallit kaagiat. It means Greenlanders' cake. It's like a bread/cake. We slice it up and eat it with butter, mainly on gatherings with family and friends. Hope you enjoy.

In the summertime the sun is up day and night. We really enjoy it, and sometimes we forget what time it is. In the summer many people spend their time outside: fishing, hunting or spending time in their cabins in the nature. And in August and September we collect berries in the nature. We call them *paarnat*, like my name Paarnaq.

In the winter it is very cold and very dark outside. And where I live in Nuuk it gets dark around three and four o'clock in the afternoon. So we can see the Northern Lights almost every day. And when we whistle they move. There is a myth about the Northern Lights that says if you whistle at them they will come and cut your head off and use it as a football. When we were children we always was so afraid to whistle at them. Funny ☺

I was born in a little town called Narsaq in South Greenland, and we have South Greenland trees. Actually to be precise there are trees in Narsarsuaq and we also have a lot of bushes and some of them get very tall, almost like smaller trees.

In South Greenland there are many sheep farm-ers, living out of their sheep and crops, potatoes, salats, beets, flowers, and in North Greenland there are many hunters living out of their catch: seals, whales, reindeer, muskox and fish.

And in the middle of Greenland we have the main place Nuuk where I live. It's like any other city. We have a cinema, swimming pool, shopping centre and so on. We live very modern, although there are only around 16,500 people in Nuuk.

I hope you got enough information and good luck with your project.

Best wishes,

Paarnaq, 22 years old

Recipe for Kalaallit Kaagiat

500ml water
25g yeast
500g flour
100g sugar
100g raisins

100g butter
½ teaspoon salt

Melt the yeast in warm water then mix the remaining ingredients.
Leave it to rest for 30 minutes.
Heat the oven to 200° Celsius. When it's done resting, shape it like bread, baste the top with milk or eggs and then bake it for 30–45 minutes.
When it's done baking, cool it down and enjoy it with butter.

Ontario, Canada

Chris Hadfield had just recently returned from
his mission on the International Space Station when
Toby's project started, and when he published his book
Sabine bought the grown-up version and Toby got the
children's version. When Toby said that he wanted to
write to him, we didn't have much hope, but we emailed
nonetheless. We received a very friendly response and an
invitation for Toby to send his letter. Toby was thrilled to
receive a letter from somebody who had been on the
International Space Station and since then is in search
of a way to get one of his actual letters into space!

Letter to Chris

Dear Chris,
How are you? What is your favourite photo that you have taken? What was your favourite song to play on the guitar in space? When you had 16 sunrises and 16 sunsets in a day, were they all the same? What is it like commanding a space station? Were you ever scared in space? What would happen if you made a mistake with the scientific experiments? What food do you eat in space?
    Bye,
    Toby

Response from Chris

Dear Toby,
I hope this letter finds you well. I'm sorry my letter was so long delayed; my understanding is you've turned 7 since sending your letter to me so let me offer you a belated Happy Birthday!
    When I was on the ISS I was fortunate enough to take so many photos that picking only one as a favourite would be too hard. What I can say is that

my favourite kind of photo I took while I was there are the ones that capture huge swaths of Earth where you can see large parts of whole countries, plus the horizon, and beyond that the entirety of the universe. I found that view truly mesmerizing! I think for my favourite song I would have to say the adaptation of 'Space Oddity' because of the huge impact it had in generating renewed interest in space and exploration around the world. My hope is that it will motivate young people to pursue sciences in their education when they see that doing so doesn't mean you're sacrificing fun or creativity in the workplace – no matter where that place may be!

When you're on Station seeing those 16 sunrises a day, they're actually all slightly different since your perspective changes based on the ISS orbital path; one of the best parts is actually that you're getting 16 unique sunrises every day!

Commanding the ISS is a lot like being a parent. It is a LOT of work and there is a lot of responsibility but it is also very rewarding. You are solely responsible for the safety of the crew and the Station so it can be a lot to handle but the various space agencies around the world put a tremendous amount of time and effort into training every crew member, so whether you are a commander or a regular crew member you are absolutely ready for any issue or problem you may encounter, so being scared isn't ever a concern. Even when we had the ammonia leak right at the end of Expedition 35 there was no point that any of us were scared. We all knew we had important jobs to do and you are so hyper-focused on the task at hand, and have spent so many years training and preparing, that fear never enters your mind.

Most of the food we eat on Station are de-hydrated versions of food you might eat on Earth; we just have to rehydrate it first (add water back into it). One of my favourite treats on Station was a burrito with honey and peanut butter; it doesn't sound like much but when you're cut off from all your usual favourites it can be quite the delicacy!

I hope that answers all of your questions, Toby, and that overall your letter project is going smoothly!

Sincerely,

Col. Chris Hadfield, Astronaut, Ret'd

Vatican City

This was one of the very few unsolicited letters Toby sent after we spent ages trying to find a contact in the Vatican. Toby had some very tricky questions for Pope Francis, and although he received no answers to these questions he was amazed that he got a response at all!

Letter to the Pope

Your Holiness,

How are you? My name is Toby and I am 5 years old. I am writing to somebody in every country in the world, to learn about the world, help people understand each other and make the world a better place. What is it like being the Pope? How do you know that God is there? Is it OK not to believe in God if you are a good person? Do you miss Argentina?

Bye,

Toby

Response from the Vatican

His Holiness Pope Francis was pleased to receive your kind letter and he has asked me to thank you.

The Holy Father will remember you and your family in his prayers. He invokes upon you God's abundant blessings.

Monsignor Peter B. Wells

Assessor

South Africa

This is the only letter in the entire book without a response. It is also a letter that is very unusual for Toby, in that he does not ask any questions. In autumn 2013, just before his sixth birthday, Toby became interested in the lives of Rosa Parks, Martin Luther King Jr. and Nelson Mandela. Together, we read child-appropriate books about their lives, including the children's version of Nelson Mandela's autobiography Long Walk to Freedom. *After reading it, Toby said that he wanted to write to Nelson Mandela, to thank him for all he had done for the world. Sabine explained that Nelson Mandela was very sick and that he most likely would not get a response, but Toby decided that this didn't matter. For once, he didn't have any questions – he just wanted to say 'thank you'.*

Letter to Nelson Mandela

Dear Mr Mandela,

How are you? My name is Toby and I am 5 years old. I like the book that you wrote about your life. Thank you for making the world a better place. I am writing to every country in the world so everyone understands each other better. I am learning lots about the world, and maybe one day I can make the world an even better place. I am sorry you are not well. I hope you feel better soon.

Bye,
Toby

Acknowledgements

Thank you to my mum, who is the best mum in the world.

Toby

There are literally thousands of people who have helped to make Toby's project happen. Rather than thanking individuals, which would be really hard, and we are scared we would forget somebody, we would like to thank all of you. Whether you volunteered your address, helped Toby find a contact, shared your life via Facebook, or sent a message that told us Toby's project touched your heart and made you happy – thank you! One person we do have to thank is Alison Hawes – if she hadn't written the book *A Letter to New Zealand*, Toby might never have thought of writing to the world. A big thank you also needs to go to ShelterBox for the work they do, and for allowing Toby to 'adopt' them as his charity, and to everybody out there who believed in Toby when he was five years old and insisted he wanted to 'make the world a better place'.